A SHITE HISTORY OF NEARLY EVERYTHING

A SHITE HISTORY OF NEARLY EVERYTHING

A. PARODY

Michael O'Mara Books Limited

First published in Great Britain in 2005 by
Michael O'Mara Books Limited
9 Lion Yard
Tremadoc Road
London SW4 7NQ

This paperback edition first published in 2007

A CIP catalogue record for this book is available from the British Library

Papers used by Michael O'Mara Books Limited are natural, recyclable
products made from wood grown in sustainable forests. The manufacturing
processes conform to the environmental regulations of the country of origin.

ISBN 978-1-84317-275-8

10 9 8 7 6 5 4 3 2 1

www.mombooks.com

Designed and typeset by Design 23

Printed and bound in Great Britain by Cox & Wyman, Reading, Berks

DEDICATION

With thanks to my publishers (although I'm not sure about their definition of this historical work as a toilet book). Thanks also to Jane for reading it first, to Gill for reading it second, and to all of you brave enough to put a book with the word 'Shite' in the title on your coffee tables. Special reference must also be made to my number-one researcher Jacquie Wines, without whose tireless work and efficient organization these words would never have made it into print.

DISCLAIMER

'Mistakes are the portals of discovery.'
James Joyce

'All men are liable to error.'
John Locke

'If the facts don't fit the theory, change the facts.'
Albert Einstein

'The man who makes no mistakes does not usually
make anything.'
Edward John Phelps

'To err is human, to forgive, divine.'
Alexander Pope

'Get your facts first and then you can distort them as
much as you please.'
Mark Twain

'It is one thing to show a man that he is in an error, and
another to put him in possession of truth.'
John Locke

'We don't know one-millionth of one per cent
about anything.'
Thomas Edison

'There are no facts, only interpretations.'
Friedrich Nietzsche

'False facts are highly injurious to the progress of
science, for they often endure long; but false views, if
supported by some evidence, do little harm, for every
one takes a salutary pleasure in proving their falseness.'
Charles Darwin

FOREWORDS ON LOOKING BACKWARDS

'History is a pack of lies about events that never happened
told by people who weren't there.'
George Santayana

'What is history but a fable agreed upon?'
Napoleon Bonaparte

'History is more or less bunk.'
Henry Ford

'History will be kind to me, for I intend to write it.'
Sir Winston Churchill

'Happy the people whose annals are blank in history books.'
Thomas Carlyle

'People will not look forward to posterity, who never look
backwards to their ancestors.'
Edmund Burke

'Indeed, history is nothing more than a tableau of
crimes and misfortunes.'
Voltaire

'Lives of great men all remind us
We can make our lives sublime,
And, departing, leave behind us
Footprints on the sands of time.'
Henry Wadsworth Longfellow

INTRODUCTION

I set out to write a book about the history of everything. After some years of savage toil, by which time my narrative had reached the end of the first millennium following the Big Bang – that is, with a little under 13.7 billion years still to go – I realized that such a project was likely to overtax even a man of my extraordinary talents. Superb as my book was going to be, it was clear that it would be beyond the intellectual capabilities, the pocket, and the physical strength of all but a handful of readers.

This book, therefore, is about the history of *nearly* everything, which is, frankly, still far more than any reader either could, or should, want to know. Doubtless, to the pedant, there are omissions, though very few and very insignificant. I do not hold to Santayana's idiotic view that 'Those without a sense of the past are condemned to repeat it,' and I have therefore left out anything that I either disagreed with, disliked for personal reasons, or found boring. (Besides, quite a lot of the past would bear repeating – provided one wasn't a slave, a peasant, any kind of footsoldier, sick, disabled, persecuted by those in authority, and et cetera.) In short, you will not find much about Canadian politics, the rotation of crops, the Louisiana Purchase, the life and work of King George V or the development of post-war Federal housing policy within these pages.

Such a sensible approach obviously brings great benefits to the reader. Gone are the days of wading through piffling Amendments to the US Constitution, and gone too the bewilderment of wondering why Caesar kept throwing his cavalry several hundreds of paces across the river. Welcome instead to the Parody Method of History, in which what is set down is directly related to its interest or amusement value. At last the reader is liberated: if he or she does not care two hoots for the Spinning Jenny or Manifest Destiny – why then, he or she shall not have to read of them. Instead, they will be entertained by a dazzling array of knowledge, analysis and wit, in a romp through 13.7 billion years of *nearly* all the world's history.

Any errors or omissions pointed out by readers will be deeply resented.

Antal Parody, July 2005

THE STORY OF CREATION I

DAY ONE – Night and Day: In the beginning . . . the earth was without form, and void; and darkness was upon the face of the deep . . . And God said, 'Let there be light': and there was light . . . And God called the light Day, and the darkness Night.

DAY TWO – Heaven: And God said, 'Let there be a firmament in the midst of the waters, and let it divide the waters from the waters.' . . . And God called the firmament Heaven.

DAY THREE – Earth and Seas: And God said, 'Let the waters under the heaven be gathered together unto one place, and let the dry land appear': and it was so. And God called the dry land Earth; and the gathering together of the waters called he Seas.

DAY FOUR – Sun, Moon and Stars: And God said, 'Let there be lights in the firmament of the heaven to divide the day from the night.' And God made two great lights: the greater light to rule the day, and the lesser light to rule the night: he made the stars also.

DAY FIVE – Sea Creatures and Birds: And God said, 'Let the waters bring forth abundantly the moving creature that hath life, and fowl that may fly above the earth' . . . And God created great whales, and every living creature that moveth . . . and every winged fowl after his kind.

DAY SIX – Land Animals and Man: And God said, 'Let the earth bring forth the living creature after his kind, cattle and beast of the earth' . . . And God made the beast of the earth . . . And God said, 'Let us make man in our image, after our likeness.' So God created man in his own image . . . male and female he created them.

DAY SEVEN – A Well-Earned Rest: Thus the heavens and the earth were finished . . . And on the seventh day God ended his work which he had made; and he rested . . . And God blessed the seventh day.

WAS GOD A CLEVER GUY?
MAYBE. MAYBE NOT

'In the beginning was nonsense, and the nonsense was with God,
and the nonsense was God.'
Friedrich Nietzsche

' . . . in the beginning, when the world was young,
there were a great many thoughts but no such thing as truth.
Man made the truths himself and each truth was a composite
of a great many vague thoughts.'
Sherwood Anderson

'On the sixth day God created man. On the seventh day,
man returned the favour.'
Anonymous

'It may be that our role on this planet is not to worship God,
but to create him.'
Arthur C. Clarke

'I think there are innumerable gods. What we on earth call God is a
little tribal God who has made an awful mess.'
William S. Burroughs

' . . . that a God like Jehovah should have created this world of
misery and woe, out of pure caprice, and because he enjoyed doing
it, and should then have clapped his hands in praise of his work, and
declared everything to be good – that will not do at all!'
Arthur Schopenhauer

'Which is it, is man one of God's blunders or is God one of man's?'
Friedrich Nietzsche

'If the Lord Almighty had consulted me before embarking upon
Creation, I should have recommended something simpler.'
Alfonso the Wise, King of Castile

THE STORY OF CREATION II

In the beginning (about 13.7 billion years ago), there was a . . . Bang. A Big Bang. Scientists used this term to explain how the Universe was generated from an enormous explosion of space and matter, in a dense and hot state. After the Big Bang, the Universe got bigger and bigger and bigger as time passed by. After a billion x 365 days it made the galaxies and the stars. After the next 12 or so billion x 365 days yet more galaxies and stars were created. So no time to rest just yet then . . .

THE BIG BANG

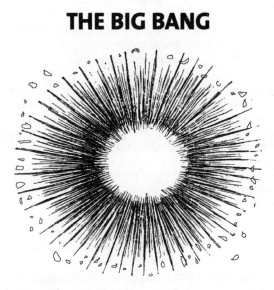

> 'I don't pretend to understand the Universe –
> it's a great deal bigger than me.'
> **Thomas Carlyle**

LET THERE BE SUNTANS

Our solar system began forming about 5 billion years ago when a drifting gas cloud on the very edge of the Milky Way slowly began to shrink and spin round. This cloud – or nebula – gradually contracted, and as it did so it got hotter. After it had warmed to a few thousand degrees, it began to separate. Meanwhile, the scorching centre continued heating up until, eventually, it exploded and there was light, i.e. the Sun.

AND THEN THERE WERE PLANETS

After the Sun (which is a star, by the way) was created, things cooled down a bit and some gas and dust that were hanging about condensed into little bits of rock, metal and ice. These bumped into each other quite a lot and mashed together to form pebbles. These grew into rocks, which grew into boulders, which, eventually, after around 100 million years, grew into planets. There used to be nine official planets in our solar system (until Pluto was downgraded to the level of 'dwarf planet' in August 2006), and should you forget them, try recalling the following phrase that lists them in order of closeness to the Sun:

Men Very Easily Make Jars Serve Useful Necessary Purposes

Mercury	Venus	Earth
Mars	Jupiter	Saturn
Uranus	Neptune	Pluto

A PLANET NAMED GEORGE?

The name 'planet' comes from the Greek word for 'wanderer'. Five of the planets were known to people thousands of years ago, as they are bright enough to be seen with the naked eye. Though people in different lands doubtless had various different names for them, the ones we use come from the ancient Romans who named the planets after several gods: Mercury – god of commerce and cunning, and also messenger to the gods; Venus – goddess of love; Mars – god of war; Jupiter – chief god; Saturn – god of agriculture.

In 1781, Sir William Herschel (1738–1822) found a new planet. He wanted to call it after his patron, King George III, but as nobody else seemed to share his patriotic views, it ended up being named Uranus, after the father of the Titans. Sixty-five years later, Urbain Jean-Joseph Le Verrier (1811–77), John Couch Adams (1819–92) and Johann Gottfried Galle (1812–1910) were credited with finding the planet Neptune (named after the Roman god of the seas) in September 1846. The last of the nine planets, Pluto, was found on 18 February 1930 by Clyde Tombaugh, the first American to discover a planet. It was named after the Roman god of the underworld – not the Disney doggy. However, in August 2006, Pluto lost its status as the ninth planet in the solar system, and was reclassified as a dwarf planet.

In October 2003, American astronomers Michael E. Brown, Chad Trujillo and David L. Rabinowitz found a tenth planet in our solar system. It was believed to be larger than Pluto and three times as far away. Its existence was revealed in July 2005 and it was given the temporary name of 2003 UB313. Later named Eris, the new planet is the most distant object ever seen in orbit around the Sun.

EARTH AND SUN

Though it is now understood that the Sun is the centre of the solar system and the planets all orbit the Sun, many found this hard to believe for a long time. In 1543, the Polish astronomer and mathematician, Nicolaus Copernicus (1473–1543), who is often referred to as the founder of modern astrology, wrote a book suggesting that the Sun was at the centre of the Universe and the Earth orbited around it and rotated daily on its axis. He dared not publish the book in his lifetime, however, and only saw the first copy of it on his deathbed. As he feared it would be, the book was swiftly banned by the Catholic Church.

A follower of Copernicus, Giordano Bruno (c.1548–1600), openly disclosed his ideas that the Universe was infinite, the Earth moved around the Sun, the stars were other suns with planets around them, and that life was not confined to the Earth. After a period of imprisonment for disseminating such controversial notions, he was tried and burnt at the stake for heresy. Similarly, Galileo Galilei (1564–1642), under threat of torture, was forced to deny that the Earth moved around the Sun, and though the Catholic Inquisition spared him his life, he was subject to house arrest from 1633 until his death nine years later. Eventually, however, the Church came to accept the validity of these scientific findings.

Enter This Solar System At Your Own Risk

- The hottest planet in the solar system is Venus, with an estimated surface temperature of 462°C (864°F).

- 1 AU (astronomical unit) is the average distance between the Earth and the Sun, about 150 million km (roughly 93 million miles).

- In 1911, a dog was killed in Nakhla, Egypt, when a chunk of Mars fell on it.

EXERCISING A BIT OF PULL

The planets are held in position by the Sun's gravity. Gravity, eh? Well, the Greek philosopher Aristotle (384–322 BC) had the idea that a body falling to the ground is seeking its 'natural place'. The Greek astronomer, Hipparchus (c.190–120 BC), who some consider to have been the greatest astronomer of antiquity, wrote a treatise entitled 'On Objects Carried Down by their Weight', while the philosopher, astronomer and mathematician Varahamihira (AD 505–587) wrote about gravity in AD 575. Generally though, in those days little attention was really paid to the subject.

The English physicist, mathematician, astronomer, philosopher and alchemist Sir Isaac Newton (1642–1727) wrote the *Philosophiae Naturalis Principia Mathematica* (published in 1687), in which he described universal gravitation and his laws of motion. People started to sit up and listen after that.

Albert Einstein (1879–1955) had a theory about gravity, too, and assumed it travelled at the speed of light. He didn't know that for sure, but he built his 1915 General Theory of Relativity around this idea and became world famous because of it. (In truth, though, that particular theory is far too complicated for most people to get their heads round.)

Pulling Power

- All matter in the Universe exerts a pull. The bigger something is, the stronger its pull. The Earth has strong gravity, but the Sun is much bigger and has more powerful gravity.

- In the absence of the Sun's gravity, the Earth would move off in a straight line.

- It was recently discovered that gravity *does* travel at the speed of light.

'Bodies fall towards the Earth as it is in the nature of the Earth to attract bodies.'
Varahamihira

10 AMAZING THINGS ABOUT EARTH

1. Our planet was formed from a ball of dust and hot gases about 4,500,000,000 years ago.

2. The Earth is not flat, nor is it round – it's an ellipsoid (it is flattened at the Poles and bulges at the Equator).

3. Nearly one-eighth of the land on Earth is desert, while almost one-fifth is mountainous.

4. About one-tenth of the Earth's surface is permanently covered with ice.

5. If you navigated your way around the circumference of the Earth, you would undertake a journey of 40,000 km (25,000 miles).

6. Oxygen is the most abundant element in the Earth's crust, waters, and atmosphere (about 49.5 per cent).

7. The Earth spins on its axis (an imaginary line between the Poles) once a day and travels round the Sun in 365 days.

8. The Earth travels at around 107,000 km (66,500 miles) per hour. Luckily they have no speed cameras in space . . . yet.

9. The Earth weighs 6.6 sextillion tons (how many noughts is that?).

10. It is estimated that sunlight takes about 8 minutes and 20 seconds to reach the Earth at 299,792 km/sec (186,282 miles/sec).

'Magnetism is one of the Six Fundamental Forces of the Universe, with the other five being Gravity, Duct Tape, Whining, Remote Control, and The Force That Pulls Dogs Toward The Groins Of Strangers.'
Dave Barry

> 'Mortal as I am, I know that I am born for a day. But when I follow at my pleasure the serried multitude of the stars in their circular course, my feet no longer touch the Earth.'
> **Ptolemy**

A STAR IS BORN

☆ Ancient astrologers could predict tides and seasons by looking at the stars and planets. An early use for astrology was for farming, as it was important to plant and harvest crops at the right time.

☆ Early astrologers recognized only one constellation – Canis Major. The Dog Star – named Sirius by the Greeks (meaning 'scorching' or 'burning') – is over twenty times brighter than our Sun, more than twice as big, and is the brightest visible star in the northern hemisphere. The ancient Egyptians are believed to have called the star Sihor, which was another name for the dog-headed god Anubis, though later traditions associate the star with the god Osiris. Its annual appearance just before dawn at the Summer Solstice heralded the coming flooding of the Nile, upon which Egyptian agriculture depended. The ancient Egyptians refused to bury their dead during the days Sirius was hidden from view, as they believed that Sirius was the doorway to the afterlife. Though many other ancient civilizations revered this star, not all were so fond of it – the Greeks, for example, held Sirius responsible for heatstroke, intemperate behaviour and madness.

☆ By the fifth century, the Chinese had catalogued 1,464 stars.

☆ Astronomy and astrology were once regarded as being virtually the same thing. Isidore of Seville (c.560–636) was one of the first to distinguish between them, but astronomy did not begin to be separated from astrology until the sixteenth century.

☆ In AD 150, Ptolemy wrote *The Almagest*, which summarizes the astronomical knowledge of the ancients, especially that of Aristotle.

☆ In his *Book of Fixed Stars* (964), the Persian astronomer Abd Al-Rahman Al Sufi (903–986) suggested that the Milky Way is made up of countless stars. This would be proven 500 years later, with the invention of the telescope.

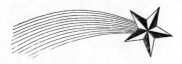

Astronomical Numbers

- The majority of galaxies are moving away from us. When we look into distant space, we are looking at the past.

- Even the nearest star is over 270,000 times further away than the Sun.

- The cosmos contains approximately 50,000,000,000 galaxies.

- There are between 100,000,000,000 and 1,000,000,000,000 stars in a normal galaxy.

- The Moon is one million times drier than the Gobi Desert.

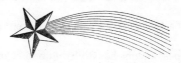

JOURNEY TO THE CENTRE OF THE EARTH I: THE SCOTCH-EGG THEORY

breadcrumbs = Earth's crust

sausage-meat = mantle

egg white = outer core

egg yolk = inner core

'The marble, the schist, the calcaeous rocks, the red sandstone, had disappeared, leaving in their places a dark and gloomy wall, sombre and without brightness. When we reached a remarkably narrow part of the tunnel, I leaned my left hand against the rock. When I took my hand away, and happened to glance at it, it was quite black. We had reached the coal strata of the Central Earth.'
Journey to the Centre of the Earth, **Jules Verne**

JOURNEY TO THE CENTRE OF THE EARTH II: YOU'RE GOING DOWN

It is about 6,400 km (4,000 miles) to the centre of the Earth.

The deepest anyone has drilled into the Earth is around 12 kilometres (7.5 miles).

The deeper into the Earth you go, the higher the temperature and pressure. The core temperature is believed to be an incredible 5,000–6,000°C (9,000–10,000°F).

Due to massive pressure, which causes particles to squeeze closer together, the centre of the Earth is solid – it's made of iron and nickel.

THE EARTH UNEARTHED

10 million bacteria live in a gram (0.4 oz) of ordinary soil.

In a single square metre (10.75 square feet) of soil you may find 1,000
each of ants, spiders, wood lice and beetles; 2,000 each of earthworms,
millipedes and centipedes; 8,000 slugs and snails; 20,000 pot worms,
40,000 springtails, 120,000 mites, and 12 million nematodes.

The dry surface area of the Earth has been estimated at 92.5 million
square kilometres (57.5 million square miles) – that can't have been
easy to measure!

Marcus Cato (234–149 BC), a Roman statesman and agriculturalist, is
believed to have developed the first recorded formula for making
compost. To help improve soil fertility throughout the Roman Empire
he insisted that all natural raw materials such as animal manure and
plant vegetation be composted.

Today, the United States loses over 3 billion tons of topsoil every year.

AN ABORIGINE CREATION STORY

Once the Earth was without features or life. Waking time and sleeping time were the same. There were only hollows on the surface of the Earth that, one day, would become waterholes. Beneath the Earth's crust were the stars and the sky, the Sun and the Moon, as well as all the forms of life, all asleep. Then came a time when time itself split apart, and sleeping time separated from waking time. This moment was the Dreamtime. The Sun rose through the surface of the Earth and shone warm rays onto the hollows, which became waterholes. Under each waterhole lay an Ancestor, an ancient man or woman who had been asleep through the ages. The Sun filled the bodies of each Ancestor with light and life, and the Ancestors began to give birth to children. Their children were all the living things of the world. Rising from the waterholes, the Ancestors saw the creatures they had made from their own bodies and sang out with joy – each naming their creation. The Ancestors sang their way all around the world. Then they returned into the Earth to sleep.

AN INUIT CREATION STORY

At the beginning of the world there were giants who lived on the fruits of the land. One year, a baby girl was born named Sedna, who became big and strong very quickly, until, in no time at all, she was bigger than her giant parents. Soon there were not enough plants on the land to satisfy her appetite, and one night she began to gnaw on her parents' legs. With a great struggle they bundled Sedna up in a blanket and carried her to their canoe. It was dark, but they paddled out to sea by the light of the Moon. When they reached the middle of the ocean, they pushed Sedna overboard into the icy waters. They were filled with shame at what they had done to their own daughter, but before they reached the shore, their canoe stopped and Sedna's hands reached out of the water and rocked the canoe from side to side. To save themselves, the giants chopped off Sedna's fingers, and as her fingers fell into the ocean they changed into a whale, a seal, a walrus, a salmon and other creatures of the sea. Fingerless Sedna drifted through shoals of fish to the bottom of the ocean. There the fishes built her an underwater tent. Above her, the cold waters formed a crust of ice and sealed her in the wintry, watery world. And there she lives still, and whenever the Inuit are short of food, they call on her and she provides it.

MOTHER EARTH

The Greeks believed that Gaia was the mother of the Universe – without the help of a mate she gave birth to Uranus (the Universe), whom she later married. After that she just carried on giving birth . . .

'Some of us still get all weepy when we think about the Gaia Hypothesis, the idea that Earth is a big furry goddess-creature who resembles everybody's mom in that she knows what's best for us. But if you look at the historical record – Krakatoa, Mount Vesuvius, Hurricane Charley, poison ivy, and so forth down the ages – you have to ask yourself: whose side is she on, anyway?'
Barbara Ehrenreich

EARTHY THOUGHTS

'There is enough for all. The Earth is a generous mother; she will provide in plentiful abundance food for all her children if they will but cultivate her soil in justice and in peace.'
Bourke Coekran

'How far must suffering and misery go before we see that even in the day of vast cities and powerful machines, the good Earth is our mother and that if we destroy her, we destroy ourselves?'
Paul Bigelow Sears

'The Earth and its resources belong of right to its people.'
Gifford Pinchot

ACTS OF GOD I: EARTHQUAKES

In 226 BC, a massive earthquake destroyed the Colossus of Rhodes (one of the seven ancient wonders of the world) and the city of Kameiros on the island of Rhodes.

In AD 526, a quake that was followed by a terrible fire, devastated the city of Antioch (Antakya in modern-day Turkey), with the result that as many as 300,000 people perished. Previous earthquakes in Antioch had been blamed on the Christians; indeed, the city's one-time bishop, Ignatius, had been tried, convicted and thrown to wild animals in the Colosseum. This time blame fell upon Justion I, then occupier of the Byzantine throne.

At an unknown time during the fourteenth century, an earthquake destroyed the Pharos of Alexandria, a lighthouse standing 122 metres (400 feet) high. (This was the sixth of the seven ancient wonders of the world to be destroyed, leaving only the Pyramids.)

The world's most lethal earthquake struck the Chinese city of Shaanzi in 1556. It was felt over half of China and an area of some 800 square kilometres (500 square miles) was destroyed. It claimed the lives of an estimated 830,000 people and has been called the greatest natural disaster in human history.

In 1775, a huge earthquake struck Lisbon in Portugal. It was followed by more shocks, fires and a tsunami. Between 60,000–70,000 people were killed.

In December 1811, the town of New Madrid (in Missouri, USA) was rocked by a huge earthquake. The quake was so big that it rang church bells in Washington, D.C. – 1,000 km (621 miles) away. It is considered to be the worst earthquake in North America, and caused the course of the Mississippi River to be temporarily reversed.

In 1884, the Essex town of Colchester, in England, was at the epicentre of a devastating earthquake that lasted for about twenty seconds and killed five people.

The 1976 Tangshan earthquake in China was the most destructive quake of modern times, killing an estimated 255,000 people, though two or three times that number may have actually died.

Knee Tremblers

- An earthquake is a series of shock waves that develop at a point (called the 'focus') within the crust or mantle of the Earth. It is caused by the movement of rocks on a fault plane, which leads to the release of stored strain energy in the rocks.

- People once believed that earthquakes occurred when Atlas, the mythological Titan doomed to bear the world on his back, shrugged his shoulders.

- The Greek philosopher Aristotle recognized as early as 350 BC that soft ground shakes more than hard rock during an earthquake.

- The great Chinese scholar Zhang Heng (AD 78–139) invented the first seismograph.

- In his treatise on the causes of natural phenomena, the philosopher Seneca the Younger (c.5 BC–AD 65), adviser to the Emperor Nero, included an entire book on earthquakes. Seneca regarded it as likely that earthquakes in different parts of the world were interconnected, and thought that they were linked to stormy weather.

- The Richter magnitude scale was developed in 1935 by Charles F. Richter (1900–85) of the California Institute of Technology as a mathematical device to compare the sizes of earthquakes.

- After the devastating Armenian earthquake in 1988, the Soviet Union accepted US aid for the first time since the Second World War.

'It is a bitter and humiliating thing to see works, which have cost men so much time and labour, overthrown in one minute; yet compassion for the inhabitants is almost instantly forgotten, from the interest excited in finding that state of things produced in a moment of time, which one is accustomed to attribute to a succession of ages.'
Charles Darwin on the earthquake in Concepción, Chile, in 1835

GETTING THE DRIFT – OR MAYBE NOT

In a 1908 lecture, the American geologist Frank Bursley Taylor (1860–1938) theorized that the positions of the continents on the Earth's surface have changed considerably over the years.

In 1912, the German meteorologist and geophysicist Alfred Wegener (1880–1930) suggested that somewhere between 275 and 175 million years ago, all the continents were actually one vast supercontinent, which he called 'Pangaea'.

Pangaea broke into two land masses: Laurasia to the north, and Gondwanaland to the south.

The present continents began to break away from the two land masses about 100 million years ago.

The theory of continental drift proved controversial and was not generally accepted, particularly by American geologists.

During the 1950s and 1960s, a group of British geophysicists made magnetic studies of rocks from many areas and from each major division of geologic time. Their findings indicated that the continents had indeed once fitted together.

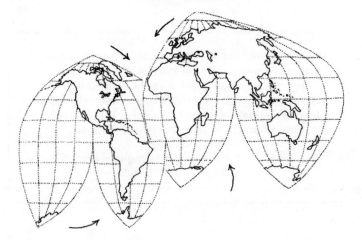

On the Continent

- Only 15 per cent of British people can name all seven continents: Europe, Asia, Africa, Australasia, North America, South America, Antarctica.

- Hawaii is moving 10 cm (4 inches) towards Japan every year.

- Antarctica is a desert.

WATER WORLD

Around 3,800 million years ago, the Earth experienced a slight cool-down, causing steam and gases to change into water droplets. And then it began to rain and rain, which led to the formation of the sea. The creatures that would later swim in it, however, had to wait a bit longer to evolve.

'Ocean: A body of water occupying two-thirds of a
world made for man – who has no gills.'
Ambrose Bierce

Rising Damp

- Scientists used to believe that Earth was the only planet in our solar system that had water. However, this idea held a little less H_2O after ice was discovered on Mars in 2002.

- In prehistoric times the sea was rusty-red. Oxygen from plant life changed it to its blue-ish hue.

- Water covers nearly three quarters of the Earth's surface. In mythology, Oceanus is the unending stream of water encircling the world.

POND LIFE

So, the first microscopic life forms (bacteria) appeared in the sea – but as there were no microscopes in those days, this is just a good guess . . . I guess. The bacteria changed into algae (one-celled or multi-cellular plants), which made oxygen – hey, we could breathe . . . although *we* would have to wait for quite some time yet before it was our turn to make an entrance on Earth. The next things to come along were creatures such as sponges and jellyfish. And then there was sea coral, followed by sea lilies and trilobites, brachiopods, starfish and sea urchins, so you had to watch where you were treading. And finally there were fish.

PRIMORDIAL SOUP THEORY –
SHOULD IT BE CANNED?

The Primordial Soup Theory is that life began in a pond or ocean as a result of the combination of chemicals from the atmosphere and some form of energy – such as lightning. This made amino acids, the building blocks of proteins, which then evolved into all the species we know today. This process is supposed to have begun at least 3.8 million years ago. It was quite a soup, but not one that Heinz or Campbell's were likely to sell.

Ingredients for Primordial Soup
Various early gases (excluding oxygen), water and a dash of lightning.

NB. Original recipe currently lost. Soup should be totally organic. The finished product may bear an uncanny resemblance to slime. Modern recipes have included methane, ammonia, hydrogen and electricity, but they are not as nourishing as the original components.

> 'The man who never alters his opinion is like the stagnant
> water and breeds Reptiles of the mind.'
> **William Blake**

LAND AHOY

When the little fishies got teeth and started biting each other, some
creatures didn't think the water was such a great place to be.
Therefore, a few of them decided to give life on the land a try. The
plants made a go of it first, then some of the fish got the idea. No
doubt the first shoalful expired on the beach, but others learned to
gulp air, and over time their lungs began to develop. Eventually,
these simple lungfish pulled themselves out of the water using their
fins, which evolved in to legs, and thus the first amphibians came to
be. And before long there were reptiles roaming (or slithering) across
the land.

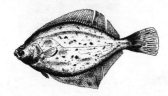

Creepy Creatures

- There are more insects in one square mile of rural land than there
  are human beings on the entire Earth.

- Each year, insects eat one-third of the Earth's food crop.

- Ants don't sleep.

- Common houseflies may be the most dangerous creatures in the
  world, thanks to their talent for transmitting diseases.

- Amphibian means 'double life', i.e. they live in water or on land.

- The poison-arrow frogs of South and Central America are the most
  poisonous animals in the world.

- Some prehistoric reptiles (cynodonts) grew fur on their bodies to
  keep warm, and eventually evolved into mammals.

A LOAD OF OLD FOSSILS

Fossils are the calcified remains of dead plants, sea creatures or animal corpses from millions of years ago, which are preserved in the Earth and sea over long periods of time. Many different specimens have been uncovered during the last two centuries, helping to shed light on our prehistoric past.

Fossil Records

- The oldest multi-cellular fossils date from 700 million years ago.

- The earliest cockroach fossils are about 280 million years old.

- The oldest known fossil is of a single-celled organism, blue-green algae, found in 3.2 billion year-old stones in South Africa.

- Ammonite fossils are among the most common; they range in size from a small coin to a dinner plate.

- It was not until science began to challenge religious teaching (some 200 years ago) that the concept of fossils could really begin to be understood.

- The cliffs of Lyme Regis, in West Dorset, England, are part of the Jurassic Coast. The area is famous for fossils, and many of the earliest discoveries of dinosaur and other prehistoric reptile remains were found in the area, notably those discovered by Mary Anning in the 1820s.

A LITTLE PALAEONTOLOGY

Dinosaurs lived in the Mesozoic Era, the 'Age of Reptiles', which began 248 million years ago (mya) and ended 65 million years ago. The Mesozoic Era is subdivided into the Triassic (248–208 mya), the Jurassic Period (208–144 mya) and the Cretaceous Period (144–65 mya). Nobody knows what dinosaurs really looked like, because we've never found one with meat on its bones. However, we do know that:

- The word dinosaur means 'terrible lizard'. The name was given to the species in 1841 by anatomist and palaeontologist Richard Owen, despite the fact that the creatures were far from lizard-like and nor were they all terrible – it was only a few that let the side down and gave the species a bad name.

- It is almost certain that the Chinese discovered dinosaur remains over 3,000 years ago. 'Dragons' teeth' were collected for medicinal purposes in parts of China now associated with dinosaur finds.

- Most of the dinosaurs were peaceful plant eaters. Only a few species preyed on their fellow creatures.

- The oldest known dinosaur is the Eoraptor, a meat-eater from about 228 mya.

- The Stegosaurus measured up to 9.1 metres (30 feet), but had a brain the size of a walnut.

- The plant eater Ultrasaurus was as tall as a six-storey building.

- The Tyrannosaurus Rex was one of the last dinosaurs to appear.

- The Dryosaurus could run at 40 kph (25 mph).

- On average, a new species of dinosaur is discovered every six weeks.

- The death of the last dinosaur and the appearance of the first 'human' were separated by about 62 million years, so there was no chance that any of our ancestors could ever have bumped into a 'terrible lizard' on a dark, rainy night.

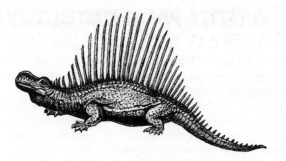

AN A–Z OF 'TERRIBLE LIZARDS'

DINOSAUR	TRANSLATION OF NAME
ALECTROSAURUS	Unmarried Lizard
BRADYCNEME	Slow Leg or Heavy Shin
CAMARASAURUS	Chambered Lizard
DEINODON	Terrible Tooth
EORAPTOR	Dawn Plunderer
FABROSAURUS	True Reversed-Vertebrae Lizard
GASOSAURUS	Gas Lizard
HALTICOSAURUS	Leaping Lizard
IGUANODON	Iguana-tooth
JAXARTOSAURUS	Jaxartes Lizard
KRITOSAURUS	Noble Lizard
LYCORHINUS	Wolf Snout
MACROPHALANGIA	Big Phalanges
NANOSAURUS	Dwarf Lizard
OPISTHOCOELICAUDIA	Behind Hollow Tail
PACHYCEPHALOSAURUS	Thick-Headed Lizard
QUAESITOSAURUS	Abnormal Lizard
RHABDODON	Rod Tooth
SAICHANIA	Beautiful One
TRICERATOPS	Three-horned Face
ULTRASAURUS	Ultra Lizard
VELOCIRAPTOR	Rapid Robber
WANNANOSAURUS	Wannan Lizard
XENOTARSOSAURUS	Strange-Ankle Lizard
YANGCHUANOSAURUS	Yang-ch'uan Lizard
ZIZHONGOSAURUS	Zizhong Lizard

COUNTDOWN TO EXTINCTION: WHY THE DINOSAURS DIED OUT

No one is absolutely sure what killed off these huge creatures, but here are a few ideas anyway:

- They went on hunger strike.
- They didn't have sex education.
- Their dinners weren't nutritional enough.
- The two that Noah squeezed into the Ark didn't fancy each other.
- They got abducted by aliens.
- The plant eaters produced so much methane that they damaged the ozone layer.
- The meat eaters ate all the veggies and then started on each other.
- The females became celibate – wouldn't you after being mounted by something weighing 20 to 30 tonnes?
- All that thumping about set off volcanic eruptions that altered the Earth's climate.
- The temperature dropped and the woolly mammoths had pinched all the coats.
- A comet or asteroid paid them a little visit causing dust and debris to block out rays from the Sun and they all got Seasonal Affective Disorder.

Possible Mating Position: Dino Style

ICE AGE

There have been at least four major ice ages in the history of the Earth, the earliest occurring around 2,700 to 2,300 million years ago. During the most severe ice age of the last 1,000 million years, the sea may have been frozen even at the Equator. The last glacial period ended about 10,000 years ago – before the development of human settlements and agriculture.

Ice Say, Ice Say, Ice Say

- The first ice skates were made from animal bones. Leather straps were slipped through holes that had been bored at each end of the bone. The Dutch word for 'skate' is *schenkel*, meaning 'leg bone'.
- The oldest pair of skates dates back to 3000 BC. They were found at the bottom of a lake in Switzerland.
- A 7,000-year-old Russian cave painting depicts the early use of rudimentary skis.
- Ice cream first appeared among the Chinese nobility 4,000 years ago, in the form of a milk and rice concoction packed in snow.
- Legend has it that the Roman Emperor Nero used to send his slaves to the mountains to collect snow and ice to use in his iced desserts.
- Sir Francis Bacon (1561–1626) developed pneumonia while stuffing a chicken with snow – he was experimenting with the effect of cold on the preservation of meat.
- Ice hockey was first played in 1885 by British soldiers stationed in Canada.
- In 1905, the Popsicle (ice lolly) was invented by an eleven-year-old named Frank Epperson.

'Some say the world will end in fire, some say in ice.'
Robert Frost

POLES APART

The ancient Greeks came up with the idea of Antarctica in 350 BC. They knew about the Arctic, which they called 'Arktos' (the bear), after the constellation the Great Bear, and deemed that there was a similar but opposite cold land mass to balance the Earth. Consequently they named that one 'Antarktos'; *ant* means 'opposite', so literally 'opposite the bear'.

The first successful expedition to the North Pole was made by Robert Edwin Peary (1856–1920), who was accompanied by an employee and four Inuit men. A US naval commander who made numerous Arctic voyages to Greenland during the 1890s and early twentieth century, Peary and his team reached the North Pole on 6 April 1909.

Seven months after the US Navy submarine USS *Nautilus* crossed beneath the North Pole, in March 1959 the USS *Skate* surfaced at the North Pole, officially becoming the first vessel to reach it.

On 14 December 1911, Norwegian explorer Roald Amundsen (1872–1928) and his team became the first men to reach the South Pole. He had initially set out to reach the North Pole in 1910, but on hearing that Peary had already succeeded in his mission, Amundsen switched his attention to the South Pole.

On 18 January 1912, Britain's Captain Robert Falcon Scott (1868–1912) reached the South Pole only to discover he had been beaten by Amundsen. All of the five-man team (Scott, Bowers, Evans, Oates and Wilson) perished on the return journey – just 18 km (11 miles) from their supply depot.

'AT LAST – HERE IS ONE OF MY OWN KIND': THE STAGES OF MAN

First of all God created Adam, but being the only person in the whole world he got a bit lonely by himself so God made Eve – out of one of Adam's ribs, actually – to keep him company, and also because God wanted to get busy populating the Earth and needed a woman for the job. Why he didn't just create more people himself is a mystery. Perhaps he discovered that childbirth is painful, which is precisely what Eve would find out too.

> 'And he said to the woman, "I will increase your trouble in pregnancy and your pain in giving birth."'
> **Genesis 3:16**

Despite the agonies of childbirth, Eve managed to produce two sons in quick succession – Cain and Abel. Unfortunately for Abel, he became the first victim of murder and fratricide (after being slain by his own brother) before he could start his own family. However, Adam and Eve's third son Seth was on hand to continue the family name (though where his wife came from is another matter entirely), and thus began the process of begetting . . . or begatting.

WHOLE LOTTA BEGATTIN' GOIN' ON

According to Genesis 5, population figures were boosted thanks to the efforts of all of Adam's many descendants, beginning with his son Seth.
  'And Adam lived a hundred and thirty years and begat a son in his own likeness, after his image; and called his name Seth . . . And Seth lived a hundred and five years, and begat Enos . . . And Enos lived ninety years and begat Cainan . . . And Cainan lived seventy years, and begat Mahalaleel . . . And Mahalaleel lived sixty and five years, and begat Jared . . . And Jared lived a hundred sixty and two years, and he begat Enoch . . . And Enoch lived sixty and five years, and begat Methuselah . . . And Methuselah lived a hundred eighty and seven years, and begat Lamech . . . And Lamech lived a hundred eighty and two years, and begat a son: and he called his name Noah . . . And Noah was five hundred years old: and Noah begat Shem, Ham, and Japeth.'
  Phew – that's quite enough of that.

FAMOUS WOMEN WHO DIED IN LABOUR OR FROM PREGNANCY-RELATED COMPLICATIONS

Julia Caesaris (??–54 BC) – daughter of Julius Caesar, wife of Pompey the Great – died in childbirth.

Jane Seymour (c.1509–37) – third wife of Henry VIII and mother of Edward VI – died soon after giving birth to the future king.

Catherine Parr (1512–48) – sixth wife of Henry VIII – died in childbirth just a year after remarrying, following the King's death.

Mumtaz Mahal (1593–1631) – wife of Mughal Emperor Shah Jahan – died during the birth of her fourteenth child.

Mary Wollstonecraft (1759–97) – author of *A Vindication of the Rights of Woman* – died of blood-poisoning eleven days after giving birth to her daughter Mary (later Mary Shelley, author of *Frankenstein*).

Charlotte Brontë (1816–55) – author of *Jane Eyre* – died during her first pregnancy, possibly as a result of suffering from severe morning sickness.

Isabella Beeton (1836–65) – author of *Mrs Beeton's Book of Household Management* – after giving birth to her fourth child she contracted puerperal fever and died a week later.

Alice Hathaway Lee Roosevelt (1861–84) – first wife of Theodore Roosevelt – died shortly after the birth of her daughter, Alice.

EVOLUTION: MAKING A MAN OUT OF A MONKEY

Some Pointers to Help You Spot an Ape

It has: a backbone, hair, mammary glands, three separate bones in its middle ear, an opposable thumb/big toe, fingernails and toenails, and it does not have a tail. Spotted any apes around you recently?

Chimpanzees are humans' closest living relatives. In fact we share as much as 99.4 per cent of our DNA with these apes. Obviously some chimpanzees stayed as chimpanzees, while others evolved into . . .

HOMINIDS

Hominids are members of the human family, which are distinct from chimpanzees and other apes. They are originally thought to have appeared in Africa about 5 million years ago, but the 2002 discovery of a 7-million-year-old skull, dubbed 'Toumai', on the shores of Lake Chad, now suggests that hominids may have been in existence somewhat longer than first thought. The biggest distinction between apes and hominids is bipedalism – that is, the ability to walk on two legs, which hominids had in common with modern man.

AUSTRALOPITHECUS

Aka: Southern Ape
Appearance: short (child-sized) and hairy
Distinguishing features: large brain
Age: 5–1.5 million years
Address: African Rift Valley
Occupation: gatherer of fruit, leaves and roots, and possibly meat
Hobbies: balancing on two legs

HOMO HABILIS

Aka: Handy Man (there was such a man, truly . . .)
Appearance: short and hairy
Distinguishing features: larger brain than Southern Ape man
Age: 2 million years
Address: African Rift Valley
Occupation: toolmaker
Hobbies: sharpening rocks

HOMO ERECTUS

Aka: Upright Man

Appearance: short and hairy

Distinguishing features: larger brain than Handy Man

Age: 1.5 million years

Address: Africa/South-East Asia originally, but moved on to Northern
Asia and Europe

Occupation: fireman and big-game hunter

Hobbies: barbecuing things

NEANDERTHAL

Aka: 'Neanderthals' – the first remains of this type of human were
discovered at Neanderthal in Germany

Appearance: funny-shaped head

Distinguishing features: wore clothes

Age: 100,000–40,000 years

Address: Europe and Middle East

Occupation: gravedigger and fashion designer

Hobbies: skinning animals

HOMO SAPIENS

Aka: Wise Man

Appearance: smaller face, lighter skull and straighter limbs than above

Distinguishing features: larger brain than Neanderthal man

Age: 100,000 years

Address: the world over – not too keen on Antarctica or desert areas

Occupation: graffiti artist

Hobbies: men used to engage in hunting and women were devoted to
childcare; now, however, man-hunting is a common practice
among females, just as househusbanding is a popular
alternative for some men

Old Folks

- The oldest known Briton was found at Boxgrove in Sussex. The remains are
about 500,000 years old and possibly Neanderthal in origin.

- The Neanderthal skull was so curiously shaped that people originally (and
for years afterwards) considered it to be a sign of low intelligence.

- During the Neanderthal period, only two out of every ten people who
survived childhood and adolescence reached the age of thirty. The average
woman probably had only fifteen or sixteen childbearing years.

EVOLUTION: DARWIN'S DOINGS

British naturalist Charles Darwin (1809–82) is famous for waking the world up to evolution, but he wasn't entirely alone in his musings on natural selection or the manner in which species evolve to fit their environment. For example, the Greek scientist Anaximander (*c*.611–547 BC) believed that marine life was the first life on Earth and that changes happened to animals when they moved to dry land, while Aristotle believed that there is purpose in the workings of nature, and that mistakes are also made. The philosopher Empedocles had the idea of chance combinations of organisms arising and dying out because of their lack of adaptation, which was a view later shared by first-century Roman poet and philosopher Lucretius, who also believed that heredity and sexual reproduction occurred only after the Earth itself had developed.

In 1859, Darwin published his theories that a) evolution did occur, b) evolutionary change required thousands to millions of years, c) that the primary mechanism for evolution was a process called natural selection, and d) that the millions of species alive today arose from a single original life form. Though he was met with a storm of furious condemnation, he also received delighted recognition from others who had been thinking along the same lines, but who hadn't liked to say so. Indeed, because his findings went against most people's religious beliefs, Darwin himself had sat on them for twenty years, waiting for the right moment to reveal all.

One of the most controversial books ever written, Charles Darwin's *The Origin of Species* – or to give it its full title: *On the Origin of Species by Means of Natural Selection, or the Preservation of Favoured Races in the Struggle for Life* – helped to shape the modern world.

After Darwin's death in 1882, it was reported in a Boston newspaper that the evangelist Elizabeth, Lady Hope (1842–1922) had claimed to have visited him on his deathbed, and witnessed him renouncing his views on evolution. However, Darwin's daughter, Henrietta, who was present throughout his gradual decline, insisted that Lady Hope's assertion was wholly untrue.

'It is not the strongest of the species that survive, not the most intelligent, but the one most responsive to change.'
Charles Darwin

SOME THOUGHTS ON EVOLVED MAN

'An American monkey, after getting drunk on brandy, would never touch it again, and thus is much wiser than most men.'
Charles Darwin

'Perhaps the remote ancestors of human beings were apes, though no evolutionist has made clear to me reasons for doubting the equally plausible theory that apes have either ascended, or descended, from humans.'
Charles Fort

'Man is a god-intoxicated ape.'
Walter Kauffman

'From the point of view of the tapeworm, man was created by God to serve the appetite of the tapeworm.'
Edward Abbey

'We are just an advanced breed of monkeys on a minor planet of a very average star. But we can understand the Universe. That makes us something very special.'
Stephen Hawking

'What distinguishes our species is thought. The cerebral cortex is liberation. We need no longer be trapped in the genetically inherited behaviour patterns of lizards and baboons.'
Carl Sagan

'Man is an ape with possibilities.'
Roy Chapman Andrews

'Evolution has developed man to such a high degree that he builds zoos to keep his ancestors in cages.'
Anonymous

'Is man an ape or an angel?'
Benjamin Disraeli

EVOLUTION? YOU MUST BE JOKING!

'Evolutionism is a fairy tale for grown-ups. This theory has helped nothing in the progress of science. It is useless.'
Professor Louis Bounoure

'Organic life, we are told, has developed gradually from the protozoon to the philosopher; and this development, we are assured, is indubitably an advance. Unfortunately, it is the philosopher, not the protozoon, who gives us this assurance.'
Bertrand Russell

'I myself am convinced that the theory of evolution, especially the extent to which it's been applied, will be one of the great jokes in the history books of the future.'
Malcolm Muggeridge

'The fossils that decorate our family tree are so scarce that there are still more scientists than specimens. The remarkable fact is that all the physical evidence we have for human evolution can still be placed, with room to spare, inside a single coffin. Modern apes, for instance, seem to have sprung out of nowhere. They have no yesterday, no fossil record. And the true origin of modern humans – of upright, naked, tool-making, big-brained beings – is, to be honest with ourselves, an equally mysterious matter.'
Dr Lyall Watson

'I believe that one day the Darwinian myth will be ranked the greatest deceit in the history of science.'
Søren Løvtrup

'The Darwinian theory of descent has not a single fact to confirm it in the realm of nature. It is not the result of scientific research, but purely the product of imagination.'
Albert Fleischmann

'Scientists who go about teaching that evolution is a fact of life are great con men, and the story they are telling may be the greatest hoax ever.'
Dr T. N. Tahmisian

TOP TOOLS AND LABOUR-SAVING DEVICES

Though we don't know what the first tool was, these basic devices certainly provided man with some much-needed help.

Flints	Hand-axe	Spearhead	Hammer	Chisel
Razor	Reaping hook	Plough	Yoke	Knife
Scythe	Lever	Wedge	Roller	Wheel

- The world's oldest tools – sharpened pebbles, to be specific – were found in Ethiopia and are about 2.5 million years old.

- The hand-axe was not a chopping instrument, but rather one that was used for skinning and cutting (animals, one hopes).

- The wheel is probably the most important mechanical invention of all time.

'The successful construction of all machines depends on the perfection of the tools employed, and whoever is a master of the art of toolmaking possesses the key to the construction of all machines.'
Charles Babbage

'If the only tool you have is a hammer, you tend to see every problem as a nail.'
Abraham Maslow

'One machine can do the work of fifty ordinary men. No machine can do the work of one extraordinary man.'
Elbert Hubbard

'Man is a tool-using animal . . . Without tools he is nothing, with tools he is all.'
Thomas Carlyle

> 'Man – despite his artistic pretensions, his
> sophistication, and his many accomplishments –
> owes his existence to a six-inch layer of topsoil
> and the fact that it rains.'
> **Anonymous**

LET THE LAND PROVIDE

At some point, after a *lot* of procreating, the human population got to be quite big and so the hunter-gatherers realized that, nice as it was to share a pot roast, there weren't enough bones for everyone round the fire to chew on. Something had to be done. So, if there weren't enough animals to kill for food, the only alternative was to produce the food yourself. Thus man learned to work the land, and to plan for months, rather than days, ahead. He also tried his hand at keeping animals, and then he discovered rivers and river plains.

Around 9000 BC, wandering people in the area known as Mesopotamia (meaning 'between two rivers', and now part of Iraq), realized that the fertile plains of the Tigris and Euphrates provided good conditions for farming. They came, they saw, they tended flocks of sheep, and they planted crops, which grew, and the people didn't see the point of moving on. They stayed put, others joined them, and eventually there was enough food for all. Civilization had begun. Many of the early civilizations began along major river systems; for example, the Egyptians settled along the Nile, Harappa culture along the Indus, and the Chinese Empire along the Huang River.

A Load of Crop

- The Aztec Indians of Mexico were the first cultivators of cacao beans. The beans were so highly prized, they were sometimes used as money.

- The South American Quechua language (the most widely spoken of all American-Indian languages) records more than 1,000 words to describe potatoes and potato varieties.

- When explorers first discovered the tomato, they were afraid to eat it in case its bright red colour meant it was poisonous.

> 'The Earth neither grows old nor wears out if it is dunged.'
> **Columella**

FERTILITY RIGHTS

A connection between the words 'human' and 'soil' may exist: the Greek word for man is *homos*; the Latin word for soil is *humus*.

Sulphur was used as an insecticide before 500 BC.

Pliny the Elder (*c*.AD 23–79), who wrote *Naturalis Historia*, advocated the use of arsenic in crop growing.

By the fifteenth century, lead, arsenic and mercury were applied to crops as pesticides, and 200 years later, nicotine compounds, extracted from tobacco leaves, were used as insecticides.

In 1939, the Swiss chemist Paul Hermann Müller (1899–1965) discovered the insecticidal properties of DDT and was awarded the Nobel Prize in 1948. Since the late 1940s, DDT has prevented millions of people from contracting malaria (it was responsible for eradicating malaria from Europe and North America), bubonic plague and typhus, although fears surrounding its links with cancer led to it being banned in most developed countries. Even though DDT remains controversial because it is persistent and lingers in the soil for long periods, due to the high number of malaria-related deaths (the World Health Organization states that malaria kills 1.2–2.7 million people each year) a rethink about the product is being considered.

Today, farmers use about 2.5 million tons of industrial pesticides every year worldwide.

Feline Fertilization

In 1888, an estimated 300,000 mummified cats were found at Beni Hassan, Egypt. They were shipped to England to be ground up and used for fertilizer.

> 'Essentially, all life depends upon the soil . . . There can be no life without soil and no soil without life; they have evolved together.'
> **Charles E. Kellogg**

THE FAT OF THE LAND: FEAST . . .

> 'Of all occupations from which gain is secured, there is none better than agriculture, nothing more productive, nothing sweeter, nothing more worthy of a free man.'
> **Cicero**

- Around 950 BC, King Solomon of Israel and Judah feasted on 22,000 oxen among other edibles in his luxurious palace – well, he did have to feed 700 wives and 300 concubines . . .

- Drusus Caesar (38 BC–AD 9), son of the Roman Emperor Tiberius, loved broccoli so much that he ate little else for more than a month and only stopped when his urine turned green.

- During the reign of Henry VIII (1509–47) it was said that nowhere was the food so plentiful and varied as in England, and that the English stomach had need of more food than others. An astonishing amount of food was consumed at court – imagine peeling 3,000 pears just to garnish the meat! Indeed, so great was the feasting that a law was passed in 1517 limiting the number of dishes that could be served, though the King himself was exempt from such restrictions.

- In 1575, the Earl of Leicester hosted a feast for Queen Elizabeth I that lasted seventeen days.

- In 1621, the Plymouth colonists in the New World and the Wampanoag Indians shared an autumn harvest feast, which became known as the first Thanksgiving.

One Hump or Two?

In ancient times, smoked camel hump was a favourite Persian dish.

> 'Don't smoke too much, drink too much, eat too much or work too much. We're all on the road to the grave – but there's no need to be in the passing lane.'
> **Robert Orben**

... AND FAMINE

'There will be seven years of great plenty in all the land of Egypt. After that, there will be seven years of famine ... The time of plenty will be entirely forgotten, because the famine which follows will be so terrible.'
Joseph's interpretation of the King of Egypt's dream, Genesis 41:29

- In 2000 BC, a major drought caused serious damage to the Mesopotamian civilization, as many people died from starvation and disease.

- In AD 1200, the annual flooding of the Nile River, which was essential for crops, failed to happen. More than 100,000 Egyptians died of starvation, cannibalism, and disease, and there were reports that children were stolen for food and graves were robbed.

- In England, during the famine of 1314, starving inmates supposedly devoured criminals thrown into jail, and ordinary citizens ate cats and dogs, among other things.

- In Japanese history, during the Tokugawa Period (1600–1868), there were 154 famines, of which 21 were widespread and serious.

- While English landowners looked on, potato blight in Ireland led to the deaths of up to 1 million people (approximately one-sixth of the population) between 1846 and 1851. By 1855, a further 2 million people had emigrated.

- During the Siege of Paris by the Prussians in 1870, starving Parisians ate most of the animals in the zoo.

- In the 1930s, Ukraine's resistance to Stalin's imposition of collectivized farming resulted in a man-made famine. In what had been known as 'the breadbasket of Europe', at least 7 million people perished when Russian grain collectors stripped Ukraine of its entire food supply.

' ... they are as sick that surfeit with too much as they that starve with nothing.'
William Shakespeare

CIVILIZED AT LAST

The people of Mesopotamia were the first to organize human society on a grand scale. They built large cities, they developed the sciences of astronomy, mathematics and medicine, and they also invented writing, money, irrigation, the wheel, laws and wars.

The huge Babylonian empire was established in 625 BC. The most famous of the kings of Babylon, King Nebuchadnezzar II (reigned 605–562 BC), rebuilt Babylon when he came to power in 605 BC, and created beautiful terraced gardens for his wife that were considered the most amazing ever seen. In fact they became regarded as one of the seven ancient wonders of the world.

The ancient Maya of Mexico were brilliant astronomers and mathematicians whose early cities thrived in agrarian harmony with Earth.

The ancient Chinese are said to have invented many things, including toilet paper, earthquake detectors, paper money, cannons, rocket technology and printing. In 1959, archaeologists in China discovered belt buckles made out of aluminium thousands of years ago, even though aluminium is generally processed from bauxite with electricity.

Pints and Puddy-Cats

- In Babylonian times, for a month after a wedding the bride's father would supply his son-in-law with all the mead he could drink. Mead is a honey-based beer and this may account for the origin of the word 'honeymoon'.

- Killing a cat was an offence punishable by death in ancient Egypt. In the event of a fire, cats were the first to be rescued. If the family cat died the head of the household shaved off his eyebrows, and it was only when they had grown back that the mourning period was declared over.

THOUGHTS ON THE CIVILIZED WORLD

'He who is unable to live in society, or who has no need because he is sufficient for himself, must be either a beast or a god.'
Aristotle

'If you are planning for a year, sow rice; if you are planning for a decade, plant trees; if you are planning for a lifetime, educate people.'
Chinese proverb

'If the aborigine drafted an IQ test, all of Western civilization would presumably flunk it.'
Stanley Garn

'The principal task of civilization, its actual raison d'être, is to defend us against nature.'
Sigmund Freud

'Natives who beat drums to drive off evil spirits are objects of scorn to smart Americans who blow horns to break up traffic jams.'
Mary Ellen Kelly

'It is our first duty to serve society, and, after we have done that, we may attend wholly to the salvation of our own souls.'
Samuel Johnson

'Civilization is a conspiracy . . . and the border between civilization and barbarism is a line, a thread, a sheet of glass . . . '
John Buchan

'What do I think of Western civilization? I think that it would be a good idea.'
Mohandas K. Gandhi (attributed)

'Every civilization that has ever existed has ultimately collapsed.'
Henry Kissenger

'Civilization began the first time an angry person cast a word instead of a rock.'
Sigmund Freud

> 'By far the greatest and most admirable form of wisdom is that needed to plan and beautify cities and human communities.'
> **Socrates**

CITY SLICKERS

- The settlement known as Catal Höyük in Anatolia (Asia Minor) had more than 1,000 houses by 6000 BC.

- Around 5,000 years ago, the world's first cities were built, including Eridu in Mesopotamia (or Sumeria), now in modern-day Iraq.

- In 2500 BC, the Sumerian capital city of Ur had a population of 20,000 people. It contained royal palaces, a temple tower or ziggurat that rose high above the city, and two harbours inside its walls that allowed trade from the River Euphrates and the sea beyond.

- The city of Babylon, Hanging Gardens aside, had huge public buildings, temples and a palace, and was surrounded by walls and gateways – each gate being dedicated to a god.

- Some people believe that the ancient city of Atlantis had technology as advanced as our own – well . . . maybe.

- Excavations suggest that the ancient Minoan palace of Knossos presided over a city of 100,000 people – this is huge by ancient standards, though Crete itself was known to be densely populated in comparison to the rest of the Grecian world.

- The fifth-century BC architect Hippodamus is credited with the first town planning, applying geometric layouts to sprawling buildings. He favoured broad, straight streets, cutting one another at right angles. He remodelled Piraeus (the port of Athens) for the Athenian leader Pericles (c.495–429 BC), planned the city of Rhodes, and replanned the new city of Thurii in Italy. Other cities of the ancient world followed his methods.

- In the sixth century, before it was destroyed by an earthquake in AD 526, Antioch (founded by the Greeks in 300 BC) had paved streets lit by oil lamps, theatres and public baths.

- In 1220, Samarkand (now the second-largest city in modern-day Uzbekistan) was one of the foremost trading centres in the world. It had even developed an early form of food preservation or refrigeration. For example, melons were exported as far as Baghdad, packed in lead boxes that were lined with snow to keep them fresh.

- In 1833, Athens was declared the capital of the modern Greek state. The city was then rebuilt and whole centuries of its history erased in an endeavour to relink it to its glorious classical past.

SOME FORMER CAPITAL CITIES

COUNTRY	PREVIOUS CAPITAL CITIES	CURRENT CAPITAL CITY
England	Winchester	London
Australia	Melbourne	Canberra
New Zealand	Auckland	Wellington
Finland	Turku	Helsinki
Italy	Turin; Florence	Rome
Norway	Trondheim; Bergen	Oslo
Brazil	Salvador da Bahia; Rio de Janeiro	Brasilia
Canada	Kingston; Montreal; Toronto; Quebec City	Ottawa
Russia	Moscow; St Petersburg/ Petrograd	Moscow
Spain	Valladolid	Madrid
USA	Philadelphia; New York	Washington, DC

'The suburb is a place where a developer cuts down all the trees to build houses, and then names the streets after the trees.'
Bill Vaughn

THE SEVEN WONDERS OF THE ANCIENT WORLD

Great Pyramid at Giza – built over a twenty-year period around 2560 BC for the Egyptian pharaoh of the Fourth Dynasty, Khufu.

Hanging Gardens of Babylon – Nebuchadnezzar II (604–562 BC) is credited with being responsible for these luxurious gardens.

Statue of Zeus at Olympia – work on the Greek monument began around 440 BC. It was destroyed in a devastating fire in AD 462.

Temple of Artemis at Ephesus – built around 550 BC, it burned to the ground in 356 BC, and was rebuilt several times until it was finally destroyed in AD 401.

Mausoleum at Halicarnassus – a tomb for the body of King Mausolus of Caria, it was completed around 350 BC and lasted for sixteen centuries until it was irreparably damaged by an earthquake.

Colossus of Rhodes – built at the entrance of Rhodes harbour, construction began in 294 BC and finished in 282 BC. It was broken at the knees following an earthquake in 226 BC, and never rebuilt.

Pharos (lighthouse) at Alexandria – built during the third century BC, it withstood several earthquakes over the centuries, but at some time during the fourteenth century the structure collapsed.

CONSTRUCTION: CHINESE STYLE

Early work on the Great Wall of China began during the reign of the first Emperor of the Qin dynasty in 208 BC, in an attempt to fortify the region against invasion from nomadic tribes. Most of it, however, was built during the Ming Dynasty, in the late fifteenth and early sixteenth centuries.

Stretching over an astonishing 6,350 km (3,946 miles) – from Shanhai Pass near Qinhuangdao in the east, to the western end of Jiayu Pass in Gansu Province – the wall was built using the forced labour of thousands of people, many of whom died during its rigorous and arduous construction. At its peak more than 1 million men guarded the Great Wall.

EGYPTIAN FREE MASONS

Located on the west bank of the Nile River close to modern-day Cairo, the Great Sphinx of Giza is believed to have been built during the Fourth Dynasty (2723–2563 BC). At a length of 57 metres (260 feet), a height of 20 metres (65 feet) and a width of 6 metres (20 feet), it was carved out of a single piece of limestone bedrock.

With the face of a human and the body of a lion, its origins are shrouded in mystery. It is not known who built the vast statue, though its face is believed to be a representation of the Pharaoh Khafre.

ROLLING STONES

Stonehenge is a circle of giant sarsen stones found in Wiltshire, England. The stones that form the outer circle of Stonehenge weigh as much as 50 tons each, and it is thought that it took at least 600 men to transport each weighty megalith. The age of the monument is not known, but archaelogists have suggested that construction took place in a series of phases, with the site as we know it today being completed some time between 2500 BC and 2000 BC.

WHEN IN ROME . . .

The Colosseum in Rome was built in the first century AD by the Emperor Vespasian and his son, Titus, on the site of Nero's palace, the Domus Aurea. It took 12,000 slaves approximately eight years to construct the vast building (originally known as the *Amphitheatrum Flavium* or Flavian Amphitheatre). It opened in about AD 80, and could seat over 55,000 spectators who were able to watch a wide range of games, including animal fights, gladiatorial combats and executions.

> 'The only thing that stops God from sending another
> flood is that the first one was useless.'
> **Nicolas de Chamfort**

ACTS OF GOD II: FLOODS

There are thought to be over 500 flood legends worldwide. Ancient civilizations all had their own versions of a giant flood, which shared similarities of plot, including the warning of an impending flood, the construction of a boat, the gathering of animals, the inclusion of family, and the release of birds to determine if the water had subsided.

After the Bible, the second most famous historical account of a global flood can be found in the *Epic of Gilgamesh*, which happens to be older than the book of Genesis. Who knows, perhaps even a little plagiarism may have occurred . . .

Scientists now think that about 7,000 years ago (possibly around 5600 BC) the Mediterranean Sea swelled, pushing seawater northward into what is now Turkey. The water funnelled through the narrow Bosphorus, and hit the Black Sea with 200 times the force of the Niagara Falls. Each day the Black Sea rose about 6 inches (15 centimetres), and coastal farms were washed away.

European explorers in the Americas were startled by Indian legends that sounded similar to the story of Noah. Some Spanish priests feared the Devil had planted such stories in the minds of the Indians to confuse them.

The worst flood in history occurred in August 1931 when the River Yangtze burst its banks. Loss of life was estimated at 3.7 million.

In 1966, the River Arno burst its banks and flooded the towns of Pisa and Florence. Many sculptures, paintings and books were damaged and the flood was described as the worst artistic disaster of modern times.

The 2004 Indian Ocean earthquake generated a tsunami that was among the deadliest natural disasters in modern history, killing well over 200,000 people. The Japanese word *tsu* means 'harbour' and *ami* means 'wave'.

Shore Leave

In 1868, the USS *Wateree* was caught up in a tsunami and carried three miles from where it had anchored in the port of Arica in northern Chile. It came to rest high at the foot of a mountain wall, two miles inland. Miraculously none of the crew was killed. Others were not so lucky, however, as only a few hundred of Arica's 15,000 inhabitants survived and the town itself disappeared – swept away by the sea.

> 'Such is the human race. Often it does seem such a pity that Noah and his party did not miss the boat.'
> **Mark Twain**

ARKANE MATTERS

Considering where and when he lived, and that he was 600 years old, how did Noah manage to achieve the following:

Collect a polar bear from the North Pole?
Collect a penguin from the South Pole?
Get a couple of elephants up the gangplank without them treading on the ants?
Prevent the lions and tigers from killing the other animals?
Feed all those animals, if not with each other?
Collect all the excrement?
Cope with the pong?
Sleep through the noise?
Float under all that weight, even?

> 'Never be afraid to try something new. Remember, amateurs built the Ark. Professionals built the *Titanic*.'
> **Anonymous**

TOILET TRAINING

There is evidence of primitive drains and cesspits dating back to 6000 BC. There were sitting-type toilets in ancient India in 2500 BC, and the people of Harappa had water-carrying toilets in each house that were linked to drains lined with burnt clay bricks. The ancient Egyptians had small rooms in their homes, presumably loos, linked to man-made channels from nearby rivers.

The first flushing toilets have been dated to 1500 BC, discovered in Crete in the ruins of the palace of King Minos. Queen Elizabeth I's godson, Sir John Harington, invented a flushing toilet in 1596. People turned their noses up at it, though. The first valve-type flush toilet was introduced in 1738 by a man named J. F. Bronde.

In AD 315, Rome had 144 public toilets. They were often used as meeting places where people exchanged news and gossip.

In ancient times, slaves had the pleasant job of cleaning and repairing all of the public utilities, while in Victorian London tiny children were often squeezed into cesspits and sewers – not surprisingly, most perished on the job.

After the ancients had been about their business, many people returned to the chamber pot. These they emptied out of windows on to the street – and passers-by. The word 'loo' is believed to derive from people shouting *gardez l'eau* or 'watch out for the water'.

In the late sixteenth century, King Henry VIII wrote an edict that made each householder responsible for clearing the sewer that passed by their dwelling, but it wasn't successful. Things got so bad in England that, in 1848, a chap called Edwin Chadwick (1800–90) persuaded the government to issue a Public Health Act to ensure that each house had a loo of some sort. That didn't help much either, because although the streets were clean, houses reeked and rivers turned into open sewers.

In Victorian times, up to 180 people used the same privy every day. 'Night-men' came to remove the waste when it was dark. Generally, drainage was so bad in cities that people were drinking sewerage.

Sewer means 'seaward' in Old English, and London's sewers were effectively open ditches flowing into the River Thames. By the mid-nineteenth century the capital had a population of 3 million, and not surprisingly the Thames was in a shocking state. In 1858, London experienced the 'big stink' during a heatwave, which led to the closure of the Houses of Parliament (on the banks of the Thames). By 1865, however, a new sewer system was in place thanks to the efforts of Edwin Chadwick, though many houses weren't connected until the next century.

Shite News

- Thomas Crapper (1836–1910) was an English plumber. He did not invent the toilet, neither is the word 'crap' a derivation of his last name – it most likely derives from the Anglo-Saxon word 'crappe', meaning 'chaff' or any other waste material.

- Both Catherine the Great (1729–96) and Elvis Presley (1935–77) died on the toilet.

- Today 40 per cent of the world's population lacks indoor plumbing.

WATERWORKS: A BRIEF HISTORY

In ancient Greece, slaves watched over the public fountains to ensure that no one washed themselves or their clothes in them – get ye to a bathhouse!

In the fifth century BC, the Greek architect Hippodamus incorporated a waterworks system into his town-planning designs, while Hero of Alexandria, a student of Ctesibius (working 285–222 BC), wrote extensively about siphons, devices which allow pipes to carry water even when the direction isn't downhill toa river or the sea.

Although the Romans made great advances in plumbing and drainage (part of ancient Rome's drainage system, the Cloaca Maxima, is still in use today), they emptied so much waste into the River Tiber that they had to bring drinking water into the city from distant springs.

Getting enough clean water into cities was and still is a concern. The more advanced ancient cities had drains under the street that carried both fresh water and sewage. Nice mix. Clean water was brought into the city of ancient Rome, but only 13 per cent of it was allocated to ordinary citizens.

In 1885, 75,000 people died of disease in Chicago after sewage seeped into the city's water supply during a massive rainstorm.

OLD-FASHIONED PRECURSORS TO TOILET PAPER

• **moss** (avoid the slimy variety) • **leaves** (best avoid the crunchy ones) • **sheep's wool** (soft, but probably not very absorbant) • **hay** (be careful which way you hold it) • **straw** (ditto) • **sand** (how does that work?) • **mussel shells** (remember that the next time you eat moules marinières) • **corn cobs** (surely they're best eaten?) • **coconut shells** (make sure you eat the coconut first) • **snow** (brrrr – brace yourself) • **hemp** (why not have a smoke at the same time?) • **sponges** (rinse thoroughly after use) • **lace** (strictly confined to royalty) • **the left hand** (wash carefully afterwards) • **newspaper** (read it first) • **bumf** (bum fodder)

RELIEF IS AT HAND

In Roman times, public latrines supplied a bucket of saltwater in which was placed a long stick with a sponge tied to one end. The user would cleanse his behind with the spongy end and return the stick to the water. Yep, there was just one sponge for all. This is how we get the expression 'getting hold of the wrong end of the stick'.

The first toilet paper appeared in China in 1391, solely for the use of the Emperor.

Toilet paper was only introduced to Britain in 1857. Despite the fact it was sold in flat packs, it was called 'curl paper'. Unlike the Romans, Victorian Brits were embarrassed to admit that they wiped their bottoms, so chemists sold the curl papers from under the counter. In fact the product was a failure at first, as was Walter Alcock's invention of toilet paper on a roll.

In 1857, the Gayetty Firm from New Jersey produced toilet paper known as 'The Therapeutic Paper'. Well, it had to be more therapeutic than a communal sponge.

In 1867, the Scott brothers from Philadelphia sold small rolls of perforated paper from a pushcart. This endeavour was a success and marked the start of the Scott Paper Company.

Soft paper was introduced in 1932, but it was unpopular initially – perhaps because you couldn't make tracings with it. Coloured paper came on the scene in 1957, a whole century after the Gayetty Firm's pioneering venture.

Strange, But Possibly True

According to a number of independent sources, occupants of the US Pentagon use an average of 666 toilet rolls per day. Though such a figure is impossible to verify, it's an amusing thought nevertheless.

IT'LL ALL COME OUT IN THE WASH

The Sumerians made soap in 3000 BC – in fact it was one of the first chemical inventions. Early soap appears to have been made from animal fats or perhaps olive oil and soda with the addition of ashes.

The Great Bath at Mohenjo-daro in the Indus Valley dates from around 2500 BC. People may have submitted to a wash as a religious rite, rather than in the desire to get rid of daily grime.

Hippocrates (*c.*460–*c.*377 BC), the 'Father of Medicine', advised cold-water baths as a cure for almost any ill.

The Roman public baths were spectacular, and the baths of the Emperor Caracalla (Marcus Aurelius Antonius, 188–217) were the most famous. In the fourth century AD, Rome had eleven public bathhouses, including one that could accommodate 3,000 bathers. The wealthy all had their own private baths.

As the Roman Empire declined, bathhouses became places of ill repute so that the early Christian church frequently discouraged cleanliness. Within a few centuries, the washing habits of Greece and Rome were thrown out with the bathwater.

The Spanish monarch Queen Isabella of Castile (1451–1504) boasted that she had had only two baths in her life – at her birth and before her marriage.

Queen Elizabeth I (1533–1603) is alleged to have said that she bathed only once a year and then 'only if she needed it'. However, this is probably untrue, for unlike others of her time, she is said to have hated the smell of unwashed bodies and bad odours.

Both the first Duke of Marlborough (1650–1722) and George Washington (1732–99) discouraged their soldiers from bathing too often in the sincere belief that it lead to the spread of disease in camp.

The washing machine was invented in 1750, but most households would have been unaware of this. Primitive washing machines appeared in the nineteenth century, but washing continued to be done by hand, run through the mangle and left to bleach in the sun.

Soap Dish

- Winston Churchill was a devoted bather. While bathing every morning, he would read his correspondence and dictate his replies. Occasionally he would have a Eureka moment, when he would leap out of the bath and walk back and forth in the nude.

- In 1950s Italy, a popular insult to use against the Neapolitans was 'Mangiatori di sapone!' or 'soap eaters', which harks back to the occasion when a crate of soap supposedly arrived in Naples, and the inhabitants, never having seen soap before, assumed it was cheese, and ate it.

'I don't like this thing of being stripped naked & washed. I like to be stripped & warmed at the stove . . . I believe it to be a gratuitous & unnecessary piece of meanness.'
Mark Twain

GET A WHIFF OF THIS

The great washed and unwashed of history all had a place for perfumes, scented oils, smelling salts, toilet water and the like. Our word 'perfume' comes from the Latin words *per* meaning 'through' and *fumus* meaning 'smoke'.

The Mesopotamians first discovered incense about 4,000 years ago.

The early Egyptians used perfumed balms as part of religious ceremonies, including myrrh and frankincense, rose, peppermint, ginger and sandalwood. Perfumes were also used in mummification.

The Egyptian Queen Hatshepsut (*c.*1540–*c.*1481 BC) led expeditions in search of incense and other valuable commodities, the results of which were recorded on the walls of a temple created in her honour.

The ancient Greeks had perfume shops, which were popular meeting places. The Greek scholar Theophrastus (*c.*372–*c.*287 BC) researched people's awareness of different scents, and noted the connection between the perception of odours and taste.

The Romans put perfume on their pet dogs and horses.

Queen Elizabeth I loved vanilla, and she applied it to everything.

Queen of France Catherine de' Medici (1519–89) brought her own perfumer, René le Florentin, with her from Italy to France. His laboratory was connected with her apartments by a secret passageway, so that no formulas could be stolen en route.

In the Georgian, era non-greasy eau de cologne was developed. It had many uses from bath essence to mouthwash.

Ernest Beaux created Chanel No. 5 for Coco Chanel in 1921. Today a bottle of this perfume is sold every thirty seconds across the world.

BAD AIR DAYS

For hundreds of years doctors thought that diseases were caused by revolting smells.

People used to live in terror of the night air, and would seal their doors and windows at night to protect themselves.

Most people's fears concerning the state of the air were unfounded, but in 1892 the oppressive London smog killed over 1,000 people, while the 'Great Smog' of December 1952 was responsible for an estimated 4,000 deaths in London.

DON'T DRINK THE WATER: CHOLERA

Cholera means 'diarrhoea' in Greek, but it has far more symptoms and is much more dangerous. It is an acute bacterial infection of the intestine caused by the intake of food or water contaminated with *Vibrio cholerae*, usually from human faeces. Early signs include fever, vomiting, and diarrhoea. The sufferer becomes dehydrated, their skin turns blue, they have muscle spasms, and their eyes sink in their sockets. An unpleasant Russian curse used to be 'May you get cholera.'

Water-borne cholera had been confined to India for at least 2,000 years, but eventually it made an unwelcome arrival in England in 1831, and in America and Paris a year later, as well as many other places throughout the world. During the cholera epidemic of 1848–9, between 50,000 and 70,000 people died in England and Wales. A further outbreak in 1854 left over 30,000 people dead in London alone.

Unaware of what caused the disease, people were terrified in their ignorance. Some even believed that doctors were responsible for it. Others drank brandy as a cure. By 1849, the Victorian physician John Snow had identified that the disease was caused by polluted food or drinking water, but no one was ready to accept this.

In 1883, the German doctor Robert Koch (1843–1910) identified the cholera bacterium under a microscope. Better sanitation and being able to hydrate patients with clean water put a stop to the disease, though it has still yet to be completely eradicated.

FLEA FOR ALL

Typhus is transmitted by body lice and fleas, particularly in places where people are in close quarters for a long period of time. Thus it is also known as camp fever, ship fever, or jail fever.

In 1489, in Spain, during fighting between the Christians and Muslims in Granada, the Spanish reportedly lost 3,000 to war casualties and 20,000 to typhus.

Historians say the high number of typhus cases among French troops was one of the reasons Napoleon's Russian invasion failed.

Fifteen-year-old Anne Frank died of typhus in Bergen-Belsen concentration camp in March 1945.

Both American scientist Howard T. Ricketts (1871–1910), who found the typhus germ in 1909, and Stanislaus von Prowazek (1875–1915) who studied it, eventually caught the disease and died of it.

A PLAGUE ON YOUR HOUSE

In 430 BC, during the Peloponnesian War between Athens and Sparta, a plague broke out in Athens and, reportedly, killed one quarter of the city's population, including the famous leader Pericles. It is thought this plague may have been smallpox or haemorrhagic fever.

In AD 165, while the Romans were fighting the Parthians, the former contracted a deadly disease that forced them to give up and return home, but on their retreat they spread the disease (possibly smallpox) throughout the Empire. The leader of the army, Lucius Verus (AD 130–169), eventually succumbed to it, which left Marcus Aurelius (121–180) as sole emperor.

In 541, during the reign of the Emperor Justinian (483–565), a terrible plague spread through the Roman Empire once more. Thought to have been bubonic plague – carried by fleas on rats – when it had struck Constantinople, the seat of Justinian's empire in 542, it was said that 10,000 people were dying daily in the city. The outbreak had killed an estimated 25 per cent of Europe's population south of the Alps by 544.

As trade improved in Europe in medieval times, so disease became more rife, and in 1339, Europeans got more than they bargained for in the Black Death. The plague is believed to have started in Asia and been brought to Europe by flea-carrying rats via the Genoese trading station at Kaffa on the Black Sea. The Black Death reached England in 1348. Forty per cent of the populations of London and the main ports were wiped out, while in Winchester the death rate was so high that the main road was used as a burial ground. By 1351, a third of Europe's population, and 75 million people worldwide, had been killed by the plague.

In Shakespeare's day, London's public theatres were closed in 1582, 1592–4, 1603 and 1607, in an effort to reduce the spread of the plague.

In 1665, the plague was back in London again and spread throughout England. All cats and dogs were killed, as it was feared they might be spreading the disease, and so the disease-carrying rats were left to roam the streets even more freely than before. Though the Great Fire of 1666 might have helped to stifle the plague in London, the death toll for the city still reached 75,000. The last English plague was a minor outbreak in 1679.

In 1855, the plague emerged in China, killing 100,000. Between 1896 and 1917, it caused over 10 million deaths in India.

Dead Interesting

- Plague is caused by the bacterium *Yersina pestis*; if the disease isn't treated with antibiotics, at least a third of its victims suffer agonizing death in five days.

- The plague bacterium is named after Alexandre Yersin (1863–1943) who discovered it in 1894 after whipping out the lymph nodes of some dead victims in Hong Kong. He took germs from these and injected them into a healthy rat, which contracted the plague. Two years later he returned to Hong Kong with his antitoxin and found that it worked.

- Rats multiply so quickly that during an eighteen-month period, two rats could produce more than a million descendants.

TEETHING TROUBLES

The Etruscans were the best dentists of early times, and they even made partial dentures with gold bridgework.

Medieval dentists thought that toothache was caused by worms in the gums.

After the loss of her front teeth, Elizabeth I feared her face had sunk, and so she stuffed her mouth with fine cloth during public occasions.

George Washington soaked his ivory dentures overnight in port.

Throughout history people sold their teeth for money. Dead men's teeth were also valuable. 'Waterloo teeth', which were taken from soldiers killed at the Battle of Waterloo, found their way into Regency dentures, and barrel-loads of teeth from the dead of the American Civil War were also shipped to England. Want not, waste not . . .

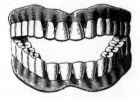

It is believed that the first known reference to toothpaste appears in an Egyptian manuscript from the fourth century AD, and describes a mixture of powdered salt, pepper, mint leaves and iris flowers.

Rather less palatable would have been the Roman toothpaste formulas that made use of human urine. The ammonia in the urine would have certainly helped to whiten teeth, but how clean they would have been is another matter entirely.

LESS BEGATTING, PLEASE

In times of drought or famine, when nomadic tribes were on the move, or when civilizations just grew too big to support themselves, a bit of birth control became necessary. Since ancient times infusions of certain plants were known to have contraceptive properties.

In 2000 BC, the Egyptians used crocodile dung as a contraceptive.

Pliny the Elder believed that a type of Egyptian wine caused abortions.

The first condoms were made of linen and were used in the early sixth century.

The Ramses brand of condom was named after the great pharaoh Ramses II (reigned 1279–1213 BC), who fathered over 160 children. (Not surprisingly the Ramses brand is no longer on the market.)

Infanticide was commonplace in some societies, as a way of keeping a growing population in check.

When girls reached puberty they were sometimes sent away from their communities as a means of preventing conception.

The Pill was developed in the 1950s by Gregory Goodwin Pincus (1903–67) with the financial backing of birth-control activists Margaret Sanger (1879–1966) and Katharine McCormick (1875–1967). It was available to women by the 1960s.

In 1979, China established its 'one-child only' rule to prevent over-population. (So now there are only 1.2 billion people living in China.)

Fascinating Facts

- Aristotle undertook detailed dissections to try to unravel the myths about fertilization.

- In 1677, the microscopist Anton van Leeuwenhoek (1632–1723) was the first person to observe human spermatozoa.

CHAT ROOM

According to the book of Genesis, Chapter 11, 'the whole of the earth was of one language, and of one speech.' When the people journeyed from the east, they decided to settle and build themselves a city, and a tower tall enough to reach Heaven. This they did, and when God came down to view their work, he was clearly a bit worried: 'Behold, the people is one, and they have all one language . . . and now nothing will be restrained from them, which they have imagined to do.' Deciding to put a spanner in the works, God scattered them across the world and confused their language so that they couldn't understand one another. The word 'babble' derives from the name of the city of Babel, which the people had been forced to abandon after being dispersed to all the ends of the Earth, and temporarily bereft of the ability to be understood.

In the seventh century BC, the Egyptian Pharaoh Psammetichus wanted to find out whether it was the Egyptians or the Phyrygians who were the first race. He therefore decided to conduct a language experiment, which involved placing two newborn babies with a mute shepherd and his sheep, and banning any outside visitors. When the children finally spoke for the first time, the word they cried out was *bekos* – which was not Egyptian, but the Phyrygian word for 'bread'. But with all those sheep about, it's surprising that their first words weren't 'baa baa' . . .

In 1493, King James IV of Scotland (1473–1513) conducted his own experiment to discover the 'true language'. He sent a deaf and dumb woman and two infants to the island of Inchkeith, in the hope that when the children learnt to speak, they would reveal the original tongue, which he regarded as the true language of the gods. The outcome of his efforts is unknown, but success was hardly likely.

The Quiet Man

We develop our ability to talk from the ages of two to six. If we have no human contact during that period we will never speak properly, if at all. The story of Victor, the Wild Boy of Aveyron, is a famous example. In 1799, Victor was found roaming in woods in southern France. He behaved like a wild animal and could only make canine noises. He was taken in by Dr Jean-Marc Itard (1775–1838) who worked with the deaf, but despite years of effort, Victor never learned to speak any recognized human language.

SPEAKING TONGUES

LANGUAGE	NO. OF NATIVE SPEAKERS	COUNTRIES USING IT AS OFFICIAL LANGUAGE
Chinese	937,132,000	5
Spanish	332,000,000	20
English	322–372,000,000	115
Bengali	189,000,000	1
Hindi/Urdu	182,000,000	2
Arabic	174,950,000	24
Portuguese	170,000,000	5
Russian	170,000,000	16
Japanese	125,000,000	1
German	98,000,000	9
French	79,572,000	35

'Great Britain and the United States are nations separated by a common language.'
George Bernard Shaw

'I love Americans, but not when they try to talk French. What a blessing it is that they never try to talk English.'
Saki (H. H. Munro)

'If the French were really intelligent, they'd speak English.'
Wilfred Sheed

'Let a fool hold his tongue and he will pass for a sage.'
Publilius Syrus

'The limits of my language are the limits of my mind. All I know is what I have words for.'
Ludwig Wittgenstein

'The English have no respect for their language, and will not teach their children to speak it . . . It is impossible for an Englishman to open his mouth, without making some other Englishman despise him.'
George Bernard Shaw

A IS FOR APPLE

Some people believe that cave paintings dating back to 25,000 BC were our earliest attempts at writing – a way of communicating an idea or information without speech.

Around 3200 BC the Sumerians were 'writing' through the use of pictures. Cylinder seals had little pictures incised on them and these were rolled on to clay, and then baked.

Pictogram writing gave way to phonetic writing, showing that the sounds of a specific language were now important, as opposed to a language that could be understood by all. Cuneiform – wedge-shaped writing (*cuneus* means 'wedge' in Latin) – developed around 3100 BC. Clerks used pens made from reeds to push the shapes into wet clay – clay was very important to the development of writing.

Egyptian hieroglyphics date from 3000 BC. The Egyptians used these 'pictures' to inscribe their temples and monuments. The word 'hieroglyph' literally means 'holy or sacred carving' and is a Greek translation of the Egyptian phrase 'the gods' words'.

The ancient Hittites, Maya, and early Cretans also used hieroglyphs, but of a style entirely different to that of the Egyptians.

The word alphabet comes from the names of the first two Greek letters – alpha and beta. The Greeks took their alphabet from the Phoenicians and called the letters *phoinikeia* – meaning 'Phoenician things'.

> 'Wherever they burn books they will also, in the end,
> burn human beings.'
> **Heinrich Heine**

PRINTING: TOOLS OF THE TRADE

The Egyptians invented a sort of paper – papyrus – made from the stalk of the river plant from which it takes its name.

Block printing was evident in Japan *c.*700, as was moveable type in Korea. During the 1450s, Johann Gutenberg (*c.*1400–68) of Germany invented the moveable-type printing press.

William Caxton (*c.*1422–*c.*1491) probably learned the art of printing during time spent in Germany in the early 1470s. The first book he printed in English was *The Recuyell of the Historyes of Troye* (1473–4), and in 1476 he set up England's first printing press. *Dictes or Sayengis of the Philosophres* (1477) became the first book to be printed in England. Since Caxton couldn't cater for all regions of the country, his printed works introduced a standardized version of English language and its spelling.

The first book to be printed in raised letters was produced in France by Valentine Haüy (1745–1822) in 1784, who realized that blind children could be taught to read by using their fingers. Louis Braille (1809–52) invented a system of embossed dots in 1829 for blind people to use for both reading and writing. In 1932 a form known as Standard English Braille was agreed on for worldwide use.

In 1755, Samuel Johnson's *Dictionary of the English Language* was first published.

László Biró (1899–1985) was a Hungarian inventor who realized the importance of quick-drying ink, and created a handy writing tool with it – the ballpoint pen – to which he gave his own name. Thus was born the 'biro'.

Take This Down

An average of 100 people choke to death on ballpoint pens each year.

B IS FOR BOOK:
THE PRINTED WORD

People first used writing to keep records and ledgers, but stories also came to be recorded in writing. Around 2000 BC, in ancient Sumeria, the first story ever written was the *Epic of Gilgamesh*. Based on the life of a real person who ruled in the city of Uruk, Gilgamesh, who was feted for his success in battle and daring deeds, became the first hero of literature.

Two thousand years ago, the Library of Alexandria housed works by the greatest thinkers and writers of the ancient world. The library was later destroyed, possibly burned by Julius Caesar as part of his campaign to conquer the city.

Ptolemy's *The Almagest* was the most influential scientific book about the nature of the Universe for 1,500 years.

Abdul Kassem Ismael, Grand Vizier of Persia in the tenth century, carried his library with him wherever he went. Four hundred camels, which had been trained to walk in alphabetical order, bore the weight of the 117,000 volumes.

10 MUST-READ TOMES

The Old Testament	Moses	1500 BC
The I Ching	King Wen and Duke Chou	1500 BC
The Iliad and *The Odyssey*	Homer	ninth century BC
The Koran	Muhammad	seventh century AD
The Divine Comedy	Dante Alighieri	1321
The Prince	Niccolò Machiavelli	1532
Don Quixote, Parts I and II	Miguel de Cervantes	1605, 1615
Romeo and Juliet	William Shakespeare	1591
The Pilgrim's Progress	John Bunyan	1678–84
Das Kapital	Karl Marx	1867, 1884, 1894

WISE GUYS I

'Drill for oil? You mean drill into the ground to try and find oil?
You're crazy.'
Response to Edwin L. Drake's project to drill for oil in 1859

'This "telephone" has too many shortcomings to be seriously
considered as a means of communication. The device is
inherently of no value to us.'
Western Union memo from 1876

'Radio has no future. Heavier-than-air flying machines are
impossible. X-rays will prove to be a hoax.'
William Thomson, Lord Kelvin, British scientist, in 1899

'The wireless music box has no imaginable commercial value.
Who would pay for a message sent to nobody in particular?'
**Associates of David Sarnoff in response to his urgings for
investment in the radio in the 1920s**

'Who the hell wants to hear actors talk?'
H. M. Warner, Warner Brothers, in 1927

'Stocks have reached what looks like a permanently high plateau.'
**Irving Fisher, economics professor at Yale University in 1929,
before the Wall Street Crash later that year**

'While theoretically and technically television may be feasible,
commercially and financially it is an impossibility.'
Lee de Forest, inventor

'I think there is a world market for maybe five computers.'
Thomas J. Watson, Snr, chairman of IBM, in 1943

'We don't like their sound, and guitar music is on the way out.'
Decca Recording Company rejecting the Beatles in 1962

'But what . . . is it good for?'
**Engineer at the Advanced Computing Systems Division of IBM,
commenting on the microchip, in 1968**

WHO'S COUNTING?

+ When man started to trade, he also needed to count. The human hand is the oldest counting tool, which is probably why we count in tens. When large numbers needed to be added up, however, things can get a bit fiddly.

− Various arithmetic systems developed, but, like language, they only worked if all parties could understand them.

x The Babylonians counted in sixties as well as tens; a counting system we still retain in our 360-degree measurement of a circle, and our 60-second and 60-minute units of time. Ancient clay tablets also indicate that the Babylonians used algebra.

= Arabic numerals were first used in India about 2,500 years ago. Numbers 1–9 were known in Mesopotamia by AD 650.

+ The zero began with the Hindus as a dot or a small circle and was referred to in Sanskrit as 'void' or 'vacant'. The Maya also used the zero.

− The Romans used seven letters of the alphabet as numerals: I = 1; V = 5; X = 10; L = 50; C = 100; D = 500; M = 1,000. It is possible that these evolved from the shape of our fingers i.e. I represents one finger, V a handful, and X could be for two little fingers crossed over each other when two hands are held up at once.

x The Salamis tablet is the oldest known counting board and was used by the Babylonians over 2,000 years ago.

= In Mexico and Central America, kernels of maize threaded through strings and mounted on wooden frames were used as counting devices from around AD 900–1000. The first real abacus evolved in China in AD 1200.

+ Leonardo of Pisa (*c.*1170–*c.*1240), otherwise known as Fibonacci, is considered to be one of the greatest mathematicians of the Middle Ages. He was one of the first people to introduce the Hindu-Arabic number system into Europe. His book of calculating, *Liber Abbaci*, which was completed in 1202, persuaded many of Europe's mathematicians to adopt the system.

– The symbol of equality '=' was originated by the English mathematician Robert Recorde (*c.*1510–58).

x John Napier's logarithms (1614), William Oughtred's slide rule (1632) and other calculating devices eased the working day of clerks who did sums for their supper, and paved the way for modern maths.

Go Figure

• In 1946, a two-day counting competition was held between Kiyoshi Matsuzaki and Private T. N. Wood, using an abacus and a state-of-the-art calculator respectively. The abacus won four out of five speed contests.

• Until the eighteenth century, Roman numerals were used in Europe for bookkeeping, even though Arabic numerals were also known and used.

• In the Renaissance, the title 'Great Art' was given to algebra. Arithmetic was known as the 'Lesser Art'.

• Charles Lutwidge Dodgson (Lewis Carroll, 1832–98) was fascinated by the number 142,857. For example, when 142,857 is multiplied x 1 up to x 6, its six digits stay the same, but their order changes each time: e.g. 142,857 x 2 = 285,714; 142,857 x 5 = 714,285. Also, when the first, second and third numbers are added to the fourth, fifth and sixth numbers respectively, the number produced is always 999 (e.g. 1+8=9, 4+5=9, 2+7=9). When 142,857 is multiplied by 7 the number you get is 999,999.

'A mathematician is a blind man in a dark room looking for a black cat which isn't there.'
Charles Darwin

GETTING IN TO SHAPE

The earliest civilizations must have had an understanding of basic geometry to build anything, though the Greeks get a lot of credit for comprehending it in depth.

It is thought that Thales of Miletus (*c*.640–546 BC) was responsible for proving that the base angles of an isosceles triangle are equal.

Pythagoras (sixth-century BC philosopher and mathematician) developed the idea of the square of the hypotenuse of a right-angled triangle being equal to the sum of the squares of the other two sides – a theorem that is named after him. However, the theorem is believed to have been already known in the Indus Valley by about 1500 BC, and in Babylonia thirteen centuries earlier.

Euclid (fourth–third century BC) was a Greek mathematician who taught in Alexandria around 300 BC. He also wrote the world's most successful book on elementary mathematics, *Elements*, which was used as an introduction to geometry for twenty-two centuries. In fact, all books on the subject pre-dating Euclid's were thrown away.

The Ancient Chinese invented the Magic Square – a square divided into nine smaller squares, each containing a number, which, when added up along the three rows, three columns and two diagonals, all equal the same number. In the example below, the number is fifteen.

4	9	2
3	5	7
8	1	6

> 'Let no one enter who does not know geometry.'
> **Inscription on Plato's door**

The Fibonacci sequence 1, 1, 2, 3, 5, 8, 13, 21, 34, 55 and so on, where each number is the sum of the previous two, was named by the French mathematician Édouard Lucas (1842–91) in the nineteenth century after Leonardo of Pisa. Many of nature's natural shapes and patterns follow this mathematical sequence.

August Ferdinand Möbius (1790–1868) was a nineteenth-century German mathematician and astronomer, and a pioneer in the field of topology. In 1858 he discovered the 'Möbius strip', a one-sided surface that is formed by giving a rectangular strip a half-twist then joining the ends together, which was an important geometrical find.

π IN THE SKY

The Greek letter pi (π) was first used as the mathematical symbol for the ratio of the circumference of a circle to its diameter by the Welsh mathematician William Jones (1675–1749) in 1706. Its value is 3.14159 to the first five decimal places. No one has found the last digit yet. Here are the first 100 decimal places, if you're interested:

3.141592653589793238462643383279502884197169399375105820974944
5923078164062862089986280348253421170679

The Babylonians found the first-known value for pi in around 2000 BC. They used $^{25}/_8$, while the Bible uses a value of 3 for pi.

The pi memory champion is Hiroyoki Gotu (at the time of writing), who memorized an amazing 42,000 digits.

COINING IT

In ancient Mesopotamia and Egypt the centralization of harvests in palaces, temples and state warehouses led to the development of a system of banking.

Shells, nails, cocoa beans, tobacco leaves, swords, cattle, horses, slaves, women – they've all been someone's idea of currency.

 The first real coins were probably minted by the Lydians of Asia Minor in 640–630 BC.

Moneychanging was big business, but the conquests of Alexander the Great brought about a large degree of monetary uniformity across much of the known world.

The use of paper money arose as a viable alternative to coins in the event of metal shortages. By the seventh century AD local paper currency was in use in China, and by 960, as a consequence of a dearth of copper for coin-making, the Song Dynasty became the first to circulate notes, which acted as a type of credit note to be redeemed for goods at a later date

In 1694 the Bank of England issued the first banknotes to be circulated on a general and permanent basis.

In 410, Alaric I (c.370–c.410), King of the Visigoths, demanded 3,000 pounds of peppers instead of coins as ransom from Rome.

Early coins were weighed rather than counted. The Latin word *expendere* means 'to weigh', from which we get our words 'spend' and 'expenditure'.

The milled edges on coins were added to make sure that no one would try to clip off the edges of gold and silver coins.

BANK NOTES

The English word 'bank' derives from the Italian word *banco*, meaning a merchant's bench in the market place.

The best-known medieval bank in Europe was the Medici bank, which was established in Italy by the powerful Medici family in 1397.

The Bank of England was founded in 1694 by a Scotsman, William Paterson (1658–1719), and the Bank of Scotland in 1695 by an Englishman, John Holland (d.1722).

The first printed cheques appeared in 1762, thanks to British banker Lawrence Childs.

The 'piggy bank' gets its name from the orange clay 'pygg' from which it was originally made. Money used to be kept in jars, which had to be broken to get the money out. In eighteenth-century England, these were known as 'pig-banks'.

The pound sign is a capital letter L written in old-fashioned roundhand with one or two crossbars to show that it is being used as a symbol. The L stands for the Latin word *libra*, the name of a Roman unit of weight, which also gave rise to the abbreviation 'lb' for a pound as a measure of weight, and to the French word *livre* and Italian *lira*. The word 'pound' derives from the amount of silver weighing a pound.

The metallic thread on Bank of England notes was introduced in 1940, and the monarch's portrait first appeared in 1960.

The highest-value bank note issued by the Bank of England was the £1,000 note, which was last printed in 1943. The £5 note is the longest-running denomination of Bank of England note: it was first issued in 1793.

> 'Gold is a treasure, and he who possesses it does all he wishes to in this world, and succeeds in helping souls into paradise.'
> **Christopher Columbus**

GOLD RUSH

In alchemy, gold represents the perfection of all matter on any level, including that of the mind, spirit, and soul.

Popular thinking associates alchemy with the quest to turn base metals into gold. Ultimately, this most tried and tested of experiments proved impossible, with the result that we are still forced to mine gold, rather than create it ourselves. On a positive note, however, experiments to produce gold from other less valuable metals formed the beginnings of the science of chemistry. Indeed, the Irish physicist and chemist Robert Boyle (1627–91) was called the 'father of chemistry' for separating it from alchemy.

One way of mixing metals to produce 'gold' was to add silver and copper to existing gold. Another was to disguise base metals to make them look like gold.

Legend had it that the 'philosopher's stone' would transform anything into gold and provide the elixir of eternal life. It was first mentioned by Zosimos the Theban in the fifth century AD, and it was not actually a stone, but a chemical.

During the Gold Rush, between 1848 and 1852 the population of California grew from 14,000 to 223,000. The gold diggers were nicknamed '49ers', now the name of San Francisco's American football team.

Between 1848 and 1965, $2 billion in gold was removed from twelve counties in California.

Of the 193,000 metric tons of gold discovered to date, 62 per cent has been found in just four countries on Earth, although scientists believe that there may be 70 million tonnes of it in the ocean.

As Good As . . .

- Sugar was once so expensive that it was nicknamed 'white gold'.

- The Aztec Indians considered red dye to be more valuable than gold.

- The fabulous country of El Dorado (*el dorado* – the gilded man) became a quest for many an adventurer (including Sir Walter Ralegh in 1595), all of whom searched in vain for this South American dream and its promised gold.

> 'Gold! gold! gold! gold!
> Bright and yellow, hard and cold!'
> **Thomas Hood**

THAT EUREKA MOMENT

Some 2,250 years ago, King Hiero II of Syracuse (*c*.306–*c*.215 BC) was worried about his crown. He was anxious that his goldsmith had ripped him off, and that instead of making the crown of pure gold, he had made it of gold and silver. Thus he asked the Greek mathematician Archimedes (287–212 BC) to determine the amount of silver in the royal crown. Because Archimedes wasn't certain how he was going to approach this task, he went off to soak his troubles away in the bath. As he got in the tub (which he'd obviously filled quite full), he noticed that water rose over the sides and on to the floor. At this point Archimedes famously shouted, 'Eureka!' – or 'I've found it!' In that moment he had realized that a crown made of pure gold would displace a different amount of water to one made of gold and silver. So, if he put the crown in water and measured the water displacement, and then repeated the exercise with quantities of gold and gold and silver, he would be able to work out whether the goldsmith had been as good as gold – or if the king had been cheated.

COME ON BABY, LIGHT MY FIRE

Wood fires and blazing torches provided man's earliest indoor and night-time illumination, but even in the Stone Age there were primitive lamps – which is just as well, considering the hardness of those cave roofs. These early lamps consisted of hollowed stone into which fat or grease was poured, with a basic wick positioned in the middle to be set alight.

By the Bronze Age our ancestors had invented candlesticks. No examples of tallow candles from the Bronze Age survive, however, because not only would they have melted by now, but peckish people actually ate them.

The early Christians made symbolic use of candles – a snuffed-out and overturned candle signified excommunication.

With regard to the lighting of candles, matches weren't invented until the discovery of phosphorus in the seventeenth century; indeed, matches as we know them today did not exist until 1834. Before that it was a case of having to strike a light with flint and steel – or rubbing sticks together if you had enough patience, and time to spare.

In the classical world the oil lamp became an art form. They were made in various shapes using different materials and were sometimes elaborately decorated.

Our ancestors understood the importance of a guiding light when entering a harbour. The Pharos of Alexandria, one of the world's ancient wonders, used fire by night to give light to sailors.

In England, the National Light and Heat Company was founded in 1812. Two years later the first street lighting was up and running.

After discovering potassium, sodium, barium, strontium, calcium and magnesium, English scientist Sir Humphry Davy (1778–1829) invented the miner's safety lamp in 1815.

In 1860, English physicist Joseph Swann (1828–1914) invented an electric lamp that predated the light bulb created by Thomas Edison (1847–1931) by almost twenty years. Edison's carbon-filament light bulb, patented in 1879, was duly improved upon by Swann that same year. The two men later went into business together.

Got a Light?

- As a child Thomas Edison was afraid of the dark.

- A rudimentary type of cigarette lighter was
  invented before the match.

- Benjamin Franklin (1706–90) proposed the idea of daylight-saving
  time in 1784. He was also responsible for inventing bifocal glasses.

- Electricity travels at the speed of light – more than 299,000 km
  (186,000 miles) per second.

- A light year is the distance light travels in a year, which is about
  9,461,000,000,000 km (6,000,000,000,000 [trillion] miles).

TOP 10 USEFUL THINGS TO DO WITH FIRE

SMOKE A HERRING	LIGHT A CIGAR
HEAT WATER	SMELT METAL
HAVE A BBQ	TOAST MARSHMALLOWS
BURN STUBBLE	BURN THE EVIDENCE
HAVE A BOY-SCOUT SINGSONG	SEND OUT SMOKE SIGNALS

> 'A horse is dangerous at both ends and
> uncomfortable in the middle.'
> **Ian Fleming**

WHEEL, WAIN AND WAYS TO GET ABOUT

On foot: Interestingly, the ancient Egyptians walked long distances in bare feet, carrying their sandals, and only put them on when they arrived at their destination.

On someone else's shoulders: Litters and carrying chairs were popular with the ancient Egyptians and Romans, and were even used in eighteenth-century Britain.

Pulled by animal: The first animal that man domesticated was the dog. Eventually man realized that dogs could pull sledges, and thus carry man around as well. In northern Europe, sledges made of rawhide, bark or hollowed tree trunks were used long before the invention of the wheel.

On an animal: Man found that donkeys, camels and elephants not only had pulling power, but were good for hitching a ride on too. For reasons unknown, horseback riding was not a popular method of travel in early times.

On wheels: It was about 5,500 years ago that some ingenious person invented a simple device known as the wheel – but no one can remember who this was. The first wheeled vehicle was the two-wheeled chariot, first used around 3500 BC in Sumeria. A wheel with spokes first appeared on Egyptian chariots around 2000 BC, and wheels seem to have developed in Europe by 1400 BC.

On horseback: One of the earliest peoples to find actual merit in riding horses were the Scythians, a nomadic people from Eurasia, who began their travels around 800 BC. The Scythians' wealth was even counted in horses. Early saddles were just folded blankets or cloth. Interestingly, there is a gap of 700 years between the use of the saddle and the later invention of the stirrup, which helped to keep a rider in his seat.

By boat: In ancient Egyptian times there was very little wood available, so the first vessels to be made were simple rafts made of papyrus reeds. Log boats were being made in Europe 9,000 years ago, followed closely by rafts and skin boats. Boats with sails were in use in Mesopotamia around 4500 BC.

Travel Details

- The first wheels belonged to potters rather than to chariots. Wheeled chariots were first raced in the Olympic Games over 2,700 years ago – although few made it past the winning post, due to the number of accidents arising from such a dangerous and competitive sport.

- Although the Inca, Aztec and Maya civilizations reached a high level of development, they never thought up the wheel.

- James Watt (1736–1819) coined the term 'horsepower', when working out how many horses could do the job of one of his machines.

- In the 1820s it was thought that the human body would collapse if our species travelled faster than a horse's gallop.

'Americans are in the habit of never walking
if they can ride.'
Louis Philippe, Duc d'Orléans

BY ROAD . . .

The Greeks were superstitious about interfering with the natural landscape and only built roads as a way of reaching places of worship.

The Persians built a Royal Road in 546 BC, stretching across their empire between the towns of Susa and Ephesus. Royal couriers could travel the 2,700 kilometres (1,677 miles) in one week.

The Roman army had stations at which tired mounts could be exchanged for fresh ones. At the height of their empire, the Romans had built 80,500 km (approx 50,000 miles) of road. They liked them straight and made to last. Early engineers even had the idea of building kerbstones and adding a camber to allow rainwater to drain away.

John Metcalf (1717–1810) built 290 km (180 miles) of road in England, despite being blind.

In 1866 the steam-driven roadroller was invented by Thomas Aveling (1824–82), a Kentish farmer.

The Alaskan Highway (built in 1942 over a nine-month period) crosses one hundred rivers and five mountain ranges.

. . . AND BY WATER

The first recorded sea voyage was made from Egypt around 3200 BC.

Until the 1800s, canals were more useful to traders than roads.

Locks were in use in China by 50 BC. The pound-lock was invented by Chiao Wei-Yo in 983, but his idea never reached Europe, where locks were finally developed around 1400. Leonardo da Vinci built six locks when he was engineer to the Duke of Milan.

The Chinese engineer Zu Chong Zhi designed the first paddlewheel boat in the fifth century.

In their ingeniously designed longboats, Viking explorers visited four continents and visited America 500 years before Columbus.

WISE GUYS II

'You care for nothing but shooting, dogs, and rat-catching, and you
will be a disgrace to yourself and all your family.'
Robert Darwin, to his son Charles

'Aeroplanes are interesting toys, but of no military value.'
**Marshal Ferdinand Foch, Professor of Strategy,
École Supérieure de la Guerre**

'Louis Pasteur's theory of germs is ridiculous fiction.'
**Pierre Pachet, Professor of
Physiology at Toulouse, 1872**

'The abdomen, the chest, and the brain will forever be shut from
the intrusion of the wise and humane surgeon.'
**Sir John Eric Ericksen, appointed Surgeon Extraordinary
to Queen Victoria, in 1873**

'Everything that can be invented has been invented.'
**Charles H. Duell, Commissioner,
US Office of Patents, 1899**

'There is no likelihood that man can ever tap the power of the atom.'
Robert Milikan, Nobel Prizewinner in Physics, 1923

'People will get tired of staring into a plywood box every night.'
**Darryl F. Zanuck, head of Twentieth-Century Fox,
about television in 1946**

'I have travelled the length and breadth of this country and talked
with the best people, and I can assure you that data processing is a
fad that won't last out the year.'
The editor in charge of business books for Prentice-Hall, in 1957

'There is no reason why anyone would want to have a
computer in their home.'
Ken Olson, founder of Digital Equipment Corp., in 1977

'640K ought to be enough for anybody.'
Bill Gates, 1981

RULERS FROM HELL

'It is better to be Herod's hog [Greek, *hus*] than his son [Greek, *huios*].'
Augustus Caesar

Draco (seventh-century BC)

Around 621 BC, a legislator named Draco appeared in Athens and codified its laws. So severe was the new legislation – even minor offences incurred the death penalty – that they were said to be written in blood. These laws were upheld for a quarter of a century until Solon (*c*.638–*c*.559 BC), the founder of Athenian democracy, abolished the death penalty for everything but murder. Such was the far-reaching effect of Draco's extremist attitude that even in modern times severe practices are referred to as 'draconian'.

Herod (73–4 BC)

King Herod the Great of Judea was masterful at building both structures and cities, expanded Judea to its largest boundaries since the Babylonian captivity, and secured favourable terms with Rome. However, he was a cruel monarch, killing all who got in his way. He murdered his second wife (of ten) and their two sons in a jealous rage, as well as his first-born son, Antipater. He is infamous for ordering the slaughter of all male infants after hearing that the King of the Jews had been born in Bethlehem.

Caligula (AD 12–41)

Believe it or not, Caligula was quite popular for a while, but after falling ill with a fever and then making a physical recovery, he was never quite the same again mentally. He had men executed without reason, fed criminals to the lions because it was cheaper than feeding the animals meat, and yet he kept one of his horses in a house with furniture and servants. Caligula forced people into prostitution and made parents watch the execution of their children. While he dined he liked to be entertained – usually with displays of torture or decapitation. He was assassinated at the Palatine Games after less than four years in power.

Nero (AD 37–68)

After murdering his mother and later his wife, Nero then married his mistress, the former wife of two of his friends, with whom he lived in extravagant style. After Rome burned down, supposedly while he sang or played his lyre (although he was miles away at the time), he built a lavish palace called the Golden House, ignoring the wants of his citizens. While Rome was in crisis, Nero went on an extravagant tour of Greece and amused himself by acting and singing on stage. The Senate was not amused and condemned Nero to die a slave's death, to be whipped and crucified. Whether this came to pass is not certain. Some reported it so, while others claimed that he committed suicide in more honourable Roman fashion. General opinion suggests that he was eventually killed.

Vlad the Impaler (1431–76)

Vlad Tepes, ruler of Wallachia, created an orderly administration, developed commerce, and strengthened the army. He also achieved the deaths of between 40,000–100,000 people, including one tenth of his own subjects. He once asked the poor and sick to a great feast and, having fed them, he had the hall set on fire and burned them all. He had countless numbers of people dismembered, burned, boiled and skinned, but he is best known for his fondness for impaling his victims, even children and babies. He was killed in battle against the Turks in 1476.

Ivan the Terrible (1530–84)

Perhaps due to his miserable upbringing, Ivan IV, Grand Prince of Moscow, became an unstable young man who enjoyed torturing animals, before he progressed to mugging, rape, and murder. After his marriage he became more stable, but when his wife was murdered he returned to his old ways. He indulged in shows of great penance for his sins, before embarking on more foul deeds including sacrilegious masses involving rape, torture and orgies, and the deaths of thousands. He once used naked peasant women for target practice and drowned hundreds of beggars in a lake. After his attack on the city of Novgorod in 1570, 60,000 people were left dead and corpses damned the river. Perhaps the only murder he did truly regret was that of his son, whom he hit on the head with an iron-tipped staff during an argument.

MAN BEHAVING NICELY: TABLE MANNERS

The words 'companion' and 'company' come from the Latin *com*, meaning 'with' and *panis*, meaning 'bread'.

Ancient Egyptian feasts often concluded with a coffin laid out containing an imitation skeleton, to remind diners to appreciate the bounteous gifts of life.

Ancient Romans and Greeks ate while lying on their sides on couches, with their heads pointed toward the table.

Medieval texts instructed diners to keep their elbows down, not to speak with their mouths full, not to pick their teeth with their knives, and not to be greedy.

In medieval times it was considered polite to throw bones on to the floor – it was rude to put them back on one's plate.

At a medieval dinner the whole table was set up from scratch, using boards and trestles, which is how we get the expression 'setting the table'. Rich households would use one side of the boards for everyday use and the other for formal occasions, which is how the expression 'to turn the tables' originated.

Stale bread was used as plates (trenchers) and after the meal these were given to the poor – crumbs from the rich man's table.

The first eating utensil was the dagger, which is why we don't point knives at people when seated at the table. However, in 1669, to make things safer at the dinner table, King Louis XIV of France (1638–1715) ordered that all table knives should have rounded ends. He was also the first person in Europe to offer guests a place setting with forks, knives, and spoons.

' . . . it is a great breach of etiquette when your fingers are dirty and greasy, to bring them to your mouth in order to lick them, or to clean them on your jacket. It would be more decent to use the tablecloth.'
Erasmus (*Treatise on Manners*, 1530)

IN YER CUPS I: BEER AND WINE

'Noah . . . was the first to plant a vineyard. He drank the wine and became drunk . . .'
Genesis 9:20–21

'The mouth of a perfectly contented man is filled with beer.'
Inscription dating to 2200 BC

'Is it the fault of wine if a fool drinks it and goes stumbling into darkness?'
Avicenna

'Once, during prohibition, I was forced to live for days on nothing but food and water.'
W. C. Fields

'I have taken more out of alcohol than alcohol has taken out of me.'
Sir Winston Churchill

DEMON DRINK:
ALCOHOLIC ORIGINS

King Hur-Aha, the first pharaoh of Egypt's First Dynasty (about 3100 BC), may have enjoyed a drink or two, as 200 of his ceramic beer and wine jars were found during an archaeological dig.

Beer, called *hqt* by the ancient Egyptians and *zythus* by the Greeks, was a drink for both adults and children, rich and poor alike.

Wages were sometimes paid in beer in ancient Egypt. Workmen at the pyramids of the Giza Plateau were given beer thrice daily.

Wine, known as *yrp* to the Egyptians, was very expensive. It was drunk by the wealthy and used as offerings to the gods and to the dead.

The ancients believed that the gods were the inventors of wine. Ancient Greece was associated with the cult of Dionysus – or Bacchus, as he was known by the Romans – the god of wine, fertility, and vegetation. Dionysus was worshipped in festivals characterized by unrestrained behaviour, the consumption of large quantities of alcoholic beverages, and orgies held in his honour.

Hooch is a derivative of 'hoochinoo', a liquor named after the Alaskan Indians who distilled it. A favourite beverage of the prospectors of the 1898 Klondike gold rush, they brought back the abbreviated version to the rest of the United States and applied it to any cheap liquor they could get their hands on.

Perhaps the most famous banquet of ancient times was the Greek symposium, a common form of recreation in Classical Greece, which took the form of an intellectual all-male drinking party that was held in well-to-do homes after the evening meal. As they drank wine, the guests conversed about general topics or held a serious discussion on a theme decided upon in advance. The only women present were courtesans, who entertained the guests by playing musical instruments, dancing, conversing, and even engaging in sex orgies.

DRINKERS' DICTIONARY

BENDER – The word has nothing to do with bending one's drinking arm. More likely it owes its name to an old British coin, the sixpence, which was commonly known as a 'bender' because it was originally made of silver and could be bent. To go drinking with a bender in one's pocket meant you had ample money for a night of serious drinking.

BINGE – Originally meaning 'soak', it became a slang term meaning to drink heavily (or soak up booze) in 1854.

HAIR OF THE DOG – It was once believed that if a dog bit you, you needed to pull out one of its hairs and place it on the wound as part of the cure (or you could eat it).

NIGHTCAP – Before the existence of central heating, people were known to have an alcoholic drink before bedtime in the belief that it would keep them warm, or at least give them the courage to jump into their freezing-cold beds.

PAINT THE TOWN RED – At the height of the Roman Empire, soldiers made a habit of painting the walls of conquered villages or towns with the blood of its former citizens, which may be what we refer to when we venture out for a few drinks, a laugh, and to wreak a bit of havoc.

THREE SHEETS TO THE WIND – The sheets in question refer to the ropes used to adjust a sail's position on a ship. If the sheets of three sails were blowing in the wind, i.e. untied, the ship would be out of control and thus it would be difficult to steer a direct course. Anyone who has tried to walk after drinking a lot of alcohol will understand the reference only too well.

TIPSY – The word relates to tipplers, who, in the fourteenth century, sold rather than consumed alcoholic beverages. Of course it's more than likely that they sampled their own wares.

TOSSPOT – A pot was a drinking vessel, from which one literally tossed booze down one's throat. If one became drunk, one probably also became stupid, slow or aggressive, which is what we mean when the word is applied to someone in a derogative sense today.

TUMBLER – The original tumblers were so called because they had a rounded bottom, making it impossible to set it down without it tumbling over, which meant that you just had to keep on drinking.

IN YER CUPS II: TEA AND COFFEE

In 2737 BC (according to Chinese mythology), the Chinese emperor, Sheng Nung, was sitting beneath a tree while his servant boiled his drinking water. A leaf dropped into the water and the taste of the drink impressed the Emperor, and thus was born the first cuppa.

In the fourteenth century, the Buddhist priest Yeisei brought tea to Japan, but it wasn't introduced to Europeans until 1560.

According to another legend, coffee was first discovered by an Abyssinian goatherd in about AD 850. The man had noticed that his goats became skittish after eating the berries of an evergreen bush, and when he ate some himself, he too felt their stimulating effect. The goatherd passed this knowledge to a monk who kept falling asleep during prayer time, with the result that the monk must have stayed awake long enough to pass on the wisdom to others.

Coffee wasn't consumed as a hot drink made with boiling water until around AD 1000. Until that time the drink was largely used by the Arabs for medicinal purposes, or was linked with religious rituals.

When coffee arrived in Venice, the Church forbade the drink of Muslim infidels. This was until Pope Clement VIII (head of the Church from 1592 until 1605) had a sip of the 'devil's brew' – whereupon he blessed and baptized it.

The first European coffee house was opened in Oxford in 1650. Coffee, gossip and the exchange of ideas were soon in vogue; so much so that in 1675, Charles II – worried by some of the conversations reported to him – issued a 'Proclamation for the Suppression of Coffee Houses'.

According to the 'Women's Petition Against Coffee', in 1674, 'Coffee leads men to trifle away their time, scald their chops, and spend their money, all for a little base, black, thick, nasty, bitter, stinking nauseous puddle water.'

In June 1767, the British government imposed a tea tax on American colonists, which later resulted in the Boston Tea Party. On 16 December 1773, colonists dressed as Indians threw hundreds of pounds of tea into Boston harbour.

Until the 1870s, most coffee was roasted at home in a frying pan over a charcoal fire. Powdered instant coffee was probably invented by the Japanese chemist Satori Kato (then living in Chicago) in 1901.

In 1908, Thomas Sullivan of New York invented bagged tea.

During the First World War, the US War Department purchased the entire domestic output of instant coffee.

The French writer Honoré de Balzac (1799–1850) purportedly died from caffeine poisoning, as a result of drinking over fifty cups of coffee a day.

The costliest teabag ever made was the one created for the seventy-fifth anniversary of the PG Tips tea company in 2005. The bag was filled with 280 diamonds and expensive limited-edition tea leaves.

Coffee-drinking was once considered so important in Turkey that a husband who refused to provide his wife with the drink could be divorced by her.

> 'The monarchy is so extraordinarily useful. When Britain wins a battle she shouts, "God save the Queen"; when she loses, she votes down the Prime Minister.'
> **Winston Churchill**

TOP 10 ENGLISH MONARCHS

King Alfred the Great (born 849; ruled 871–99) – he was strong in battle, a wise ruler, and the first English king who could read and write. He also developed the country's first navy, but he didn't know much about baking cakes.

King Athelstan (born *c.*895; ruled 924–939) – he took control of England's many warring kingdoms, and became the first king to rule all England.

Edward the Confessor (born 1003; ruled 1042–66) – he founded Westminster Abbey in London and had a reputation for being holy. In 1161 he was made a saint, but it is thought this was largely due to his wife's embellished account of his life, which, during the course of a century, had blurred the truth between historical fact and fiction.

Henry II (born 1133; ruled 1154–89) – he founded the Plantagenet dynasty of English kings, laid the foundation of the English jury system and raised new taxes from the landholders to pay for a militia force. A pity about those quarrels with Rome and with that troublesome archbishop, Thomas à Becket.

Richard I (the Lionheart) (born 1157; ruled 1189–99) – during his ten-year reign, he spent only five months in England; the rest of the time he was winning battles in the Crusades, fighting French forces and locked up in prison. Without any heirs, on his death he left his country to his unpopular brother John. Despite being the King of England for ten years he could barely speak any English.

Henry III (born 1207; ruled 1216–72) – he is England's longest-reigning king and has been described as the greatest of all patrons of medieval architecture. However, he was also weak, unpopular, and he lost many battles. He was forced to set up a 'Parlement' at Westminster, which marked the start of the House of Commons.

Edward I (born 1239; ruled 1272–1307) – he was a statesman, lawyer and soldier who formed the Model Parliament in 1295, which brought together the knights, clergy, nobility and burgesses of the cities, and gathered the Lords and Commons together for the first time. Nicknamed 'Longshanks', and also known as 'Hammer of the Scots', he is believed to have been England's tallest king. A fiercely tempered man, he once tore out his own son's hair.

Henry V (born 1387; ruled 1413–22) – he was a stern, skilful and pious soldier (but that didn't stop him from pinching the crown off his father's head before the dying king, Henry IV, had breathed his last). He renewed the war with France and in the face of tremendous odds beat the French at the Battle of Agincourt in 1415.

Henry VIII (born 1491; ruled 1509–47) – best known for his inability to settle for one woman, Henry ended up marrying six times. His determined desire for a divorce, even though it was explicitly against Catholic doctrine, led him to break away from the papacy and establish the Church of England, of which he became head, naturally. He also developed the first modern navy, and is credited with writing 'Greensleeves'.

Elizabeth I (born 1533; ruled 1558–1603) – a remarkable queen, Elizabeth was noted for her learning and wisdom, was popular with the people, and kept her court and country stable. She kept both the Spanish and any suitors at bay. She killed off a usurping cousin, but, having never married, did not give birth to an heir herself.

Kinks and Queens

- The longest reigning monarch in history was Pepi II, who ruled Egypt for ninety years, 2566–2476 BC.

- Queen Anne had a transvestite cousin, Lord Cornbury, whom she assigned to be Governor of New York and New Jersey. The colonists were not amused.

RELIGIOUS REELINGS

'The gods can either take away evil from the world and will not, or, being willing to do so, cannot . . . If they have the will to remove evil and cannot, then they are not omnipotent. If they can but will not, then they are not benevolent. If they are neither willing nor able, they are neither omnipotent nor benevolent.'
Epicurus

'But who prays for Satan? Who, in eighteen centuries, has had the common humanity to pray for the one sinner that needed it most?'
Mark Twain

'How many observe Christ's birthday! How few his precepts! O! 'tis easier to keep holidays than commandments.'
Benjamin Franklin

'A little philosophy inclineth man's mind to atheism, but depth in philosophy bringeth men's minds about to religion.'
Francis Bacon

'The Bible may be the truth, but it's not the whole truth and nothing but the truth.'
Samuel Butler

'There is a story, which is fairly well known, about when the missionaries came to Africa. They had the Bible and we, the natives, had the land. They said, "Let us pray," and we dutifully shut our eyes. When we opened them, why, they now had the land and we had the Bible.'
Desmond Tutu

'If Jesus had been killed twenty years ago, Catholic schoolchildren would be wearing little electric chairs around their necks instead of crosses.'
Lenny Bruce

'Why attack God? He may be as miserable as we are.'
Erik Satie

THE PAPACY: FIRST 10 POPES

St Peter (until *c*.64)
Linus (*c*.64–*c*.76)
Anacletus (*c*.76–*c*.90)
Clement I (*c*.90–*c*.99)
Evaristus (*c*.99–*c*.105)
Alexander I (*c*.105–*c*.175)
Sixtus I (*c*.117–*c*.127)
Telesphorus (*c*.127–*c*.137)
Hyginus (*c*.137–*c*.140)
Pius I (*c*.140–*c*.154)
Anicetus (*c*.154–*c*.166)

AN A–Z OF PATRON SAINTS

SAINT	PATRONAGE
Agnes	Virgins
Barbara	People in danger of sudden death
Christopher	Travellers
Dorothy	Gardeners
Erasmus	Navigators
Francesca Cabrini	Immigrants
Genesius of Arles	Secretaries
Hippolytus	Horses
Ivo	Orphans
Jude	Hopeless causes
Katarina of Sweden	Women in danger of miscarrying
Laurence	Firefighters
Médard	Toothache sufferers
Nicholas	Pawnbrokers
Osmund	People afflicted by insanity
Peter	Fishermen
Raphael	Blind people
Sebastian	Athletes
Thomas More	Lawyers
Ursula	Girls
Vincent Ferrer	Plumbers
Wenceslas	Brewers
Zita	Housewives

> 'The heresy of one age becomes the orthodoxy of the next.'
> **Helen Keller**

HERETICS, TREASON AND MARTYRS

- St Stephen (c.AD 36) became the first martyr after he was stoned to death for preaching the words of Christianity.

- St Peter was one of Jesus's chosen twelve, who came to Rome as part of an effort to spread the faith, and became the first pope. During this time, however, the Emperor Nero initiated a persecution of Christians, and Peter was crucified upside down c.64 and buried in a cemetery on the Vatican Hill. In the fourth century, Constantine built a large basilica over Peter's tomb.

- According to tradition, when a Roman prefect asked St Lawrence, a deacon of Rome under Pope Sixtus II, to hand over church valuables, the deacon brought him the poor and sick saying, 'Here are the church's treasure.' Lawrence was martyred in 258 – he was believed to have been roasted on a grill.

- St Cecilia of the second or third century was sentenced to be stifled to death in the bathroom of her house, after refusing to worship the then Roman emperor. Though she survived the steam, and endured three failed attempts to behead her, she died of her injuries some days later.

- St Alban was the first Christian martyr in Britain. After disguising himself as a Christian priest to allow the real priest (who had converted him) to escape, he was arrested by Roman soldiers. He was scourged and beheaded c.305 after refusing to renounce his faith.

- St Thomas à Becket (c.1115–1170) became Chancellor in 1155, during the reign of Henry II. He served the King well in high office, but after being appointed to the post of Archbishop of Canterbury in 1162, his loyalty to the Church became paramount, and conflicts with Henry were many. Afraid for his life, he fled the country in 1164, but returned in 1170 to be reconciled with the King. However, a month later he was dead; killed in Canterbury Cathedral by four knights, who mistakenly believed that the King wanted Thomas dead.

- Thomas More (1478–1535) had been Lord Chancellor of England from 1529, but he resigned his post in 1532 when Henry required clergy to affirm that, as King, he was now head of the Church of England. More had hoped to avoid a confrontation, but was eventually arrested for not swearing an oath to Henry. After a period of imprisonment in the Tower of London, he was eventually beheaded in 1534.

- Joan of Arc (c.1412–31) was the daughter of a farmer who believed that the voices of St Catherine, St Margaret and St Michael had ordered her to lead the French army into battle against the English and to see the heir to the throne crowned King Charles VII of France. Joan persuaded Charles and the generals of the French army to let her take on this task and she went on to raise the siege of the town of Orleans. Charles was crowned King in Rheims Cathedral, but Joan was captured during a later attempt to reclaim the city of Paris. At this time the Catholic Church was dominant in both France and England, and thus Joan was accused of heresy and burnt at the stake.

Burning Issues

- From about 1450 to 1800 between 2–4 million women went to the stake in both Catholic and Protestant Europe.

- In the fifteenth century, during Tomás de Torquemada's term of office as Grand Inquisitor and 'Saviour of Spain', over 2,000 heretics were burnt at the stake, though he died peacefully in his bed in 1498.

- The Spanish Inquisition burnt its last victim in the New World in 1836.

- During the reign of Mary I or 'Bloody Mary' (1516–58), some 300 Protestants were burnt at the stake.

- In 1572, Queen of France Catherine de' Medici (1519–89) ordered the deaths of over 4,000 Huguenots in Paris in an attempt to put an end to religious war between Catholics and Protestants – it became known as the St Bartholomew's Day Massacre.

'Heresy is only another word for freedom of thought.'
Graham Greene

'A cynic is just a man who found out when he was about ten
that there wasn't any Santa Claus, and he's still upset.'
James Gould Cozzens

SOME THINGS PEOPLE HAVE BELIEVED IN

Gods	Prophets	Soothsayers
Kings	Doctors	Fairies
Ghosts	UFOs	Aliens
Magic	Historical facts	The Bible
Scientific theories	Conspiracy theories	The Afterlife
The Da Vinci Code	Father Christmas	April Fools
The Earth being round	The Earth being flat	Crystals

'The Church says that the Earth is flat, but I have seen the
shadow on the Moon and I have more faith in the shadow
than in the Church.'
Ferdinand Magellan

SHAPING UP

- In 4000 BC, people thought that the world was flat. Some believed
  the Sun was a god who rode across the sky in a chariot, travelling
  beneath the Earth at night.

- The ancient Egyptian universe was shaped like a rectangle, with
  the goddess Nut stretched across it as the enclosing sky.

- In the sixth century BC, the Greek philosopher Anaximander
  (c.611–547 BC) noticed that the stars appeared to rotate around a
  pole. He suggested that the sky must therefore be a complete
  sphere around the Earth. He had also heard travellers' tales of
  different stars appearing in the skies as the traveller moved north
  or south, and thus he concluded that the Earth must be a cylinder.

- In 500 BC, Pythagoras (c.582–500 BC) taught that the Earth is a sphere. He was influenced by observations of lunar eclipses and that the Earth's shadow on the Moon is always circular.

- In 350 BC, the Greek philosopher and astronomer Heracleides (387–312 BC) made a suggestion about the daily rotation of the Earth (an idea that was not given full importance until 1,800 years later).

- Sailors had long noticed that as a ship sails away from the shore, not only does it appear to diminish in size, it also seems to sink into the water. The simplest explanation to use was that the Earth was curved. Many ships disappeared, but none were known to have fallen off the edge of the world.

- The Alexandrian astronomer and mathematician Aristarchus (c.310–230 BC) proposed that the Earth moves around the larger Sun, but people weren't too keen on this idea in the third century BC.

- The Greek mathematician, astronomer and geographer Eratosthenes (c.276–c.196 BC) worked out the circumference of Earth around 240 BC. Using trigonometry and knowledge of the angle of the elevation of the Sun at noon, his figures are believed to be between 39,690 km (24,662 miles) and 46,620 km (28,968 miles). The circumference of the Earth around the poles is now measured at around 40,008 km (24,859 miles).

On the Level

- Platygæanism is the scientific hypothesis that the Earth is flat or planar.

- There are those that still hold that the Earth is flat. Flat Earthers believe the Earth is shaped in the form of a pentagon with five corners.

'When people thought the Earth was flat, they were wrong. When people thought the Earth was spherical they were wrong. But if you think that thinking the Earth is spherical is just as wrong as thinking the Earth is flat, then your view is wronger than both of them put together.'
Isaac Asimov

X MARKS THE SPOT: MAPS AND NAVIGATION

The first city map was created in stone for Lagash, Mesopotamia, in 2300 BC.

Anaximander is credited with drawing the first map of the known world.

Eratosthenes later compiled a map of the world, stretching from the British Isles to Ceylon, and from the Caspian Sea to Ethiopia.

In AD 150, Ptolemy of Alexandria, the celebrated astronomer, mathematician, and geographer, published his *Geography,* and included a map of the world with places labelled with a coordinate grid system. He recorded 8,000 locations, as told to him by travellers, complete with his estimations of their latitudes and longitudes. His manuscripts were discovered by Europeans in the fifteenth century, and Christopher Columbus (1451–1506) and his contemporaries used his calculations to chart their explorations. Although these were somewhat wide of the mark, Ptolemy's work had a lasting influence on cartography.

The first atlas was published in Bologna, Italy, in 1477.

The Greek historian, philosopher and geographer Strabo (*c.*63 BC–AD 24), wrote the seventeen-book *Geographia* – a history and description of people and places all over the world.

Legend has it that sailors once relied on birds to discover whether land lay ahead. If a released bird returned with any sign of vegetation, a landing spot was near by.

By 3,000 years ago, seafarers had learned to read the stars. They constructed star maps and used the Pole Star to find north.

The Chinese were the first to invent the compass around 900 years ago. One type involved placing a lodestone (a naturally magnetic variety of magnetite ore) on to a bronze disk; the lodestone always pointed north. Another consisted of placing a needle-shaped piece of magnetized iron on top of straw floating on water. The Earth's magnetism would pull the needle to point north. The compass was not used for navigation at first – the Chinese preferred to use it as a feng-shui-type tool. However, within a hundred years of the early inventions, European sailors had taken the compass on board.

In the Middle Ages, sailors relied on measuring instruments (they calculated the height of the Sun and the stars from the horizon) to chart their course.

Though sailors were happy with their latitudes – longitude was more of a problem. In 1714, the British parliament offered a prize of £20,000 (worth more than £1 million in today's money) to the person who could work out a ship's correct position when sailing in an east-west direction. In 1759, after thirty years of fiddling with clock parts, John Harrison (1693–1776) invented the marine chronometer. Despite his achievement, those sitting on the prize money weren't too taken with the idea of giving him his rightful reward.

Though the golden country of El Dorado was never found, it did find its way onto maps.

Compass Mentis

- The Italian explorer Amerigo Vespucci (1454–1512) was the first person to realize that the Americas were separate from the continent of Asia. In 1507, America was named after the explorer, and the German mapmaker Martin Waldseemüller (c.1470–1522) printed a map on which the word 'America' appeared in the area formerly known as the New World.

- The first *Times Atlas of the World* was published in 1895.

- In 1947, the US sent over 4,700 men, 13 ships and 23 aircraft to Antarctica on a map-making exercise.

- Greenwich was accepted as 0° longitude in 1913.

> 'Of course men discovered new worlds. Men would rather
> travel the world than ask how to get from A–B.'
> **Anonymous**

THE FOUR CORNERS OF THE WORLD: GREAT EXPLORERS

EXPLORER	FIRST EUROPEAN TO REACH . . .	YEAR
Eric the Red – Viking (Icelandish)	Greenland	982
Leif Ericsson – Viking (Norse)	Newfoundland (Vinland)	1000
Christopher Columbus – Italian	West Indies	1492
John Cabot – Italian/English	Canada	1497
Pedro Álvares Cabral – Portuguese	Brazil	1500
Abel Tasman – Dutch	Tasmania/New Zealand	1642/1644
James Cook – British	Hawaiian Islands	1778
Roald Amundsen – Norwegian	South Pole	1911

When Christopher Columbus reached the Caribbean in 1492 he thought he was in Asia. Therefore he named the land Indies and its people Indians. Columbus's men captured many of the indigenous Taino Indians, who were sold into slavery.

Captain James Cook (1728–79) lost forty-one of his ninety-eight-man crew to scurvy (a deficiency of vitamin C) on his first voyage to the South Pacific in 1768. He was the first ship's captain to stop the disease by providing his crew with fresh citrus fruits. By 1795 lemon juice was issued on all British Navy ships.

Sir Walter Ralegh (1554–1618) bet Queen Elizabeth I that he could weigh the weight of smoke in order to secure funding for his next voyage. He placed two identical cigars on opposite sides of a scale and lit one of them. He concluded the difference in the weight was the weight of smoke. Ralegh got his funding.

Pedro Álvares Cabral (c.1460–c.1526) originally named Brazil the 'Island of the True Cross'. The name Brazil comes from a dyewood found there called pau brasil (now the national tree of Brazil).

SOME THOUGHTS ON EXPLORATION

'Following the light of the Sun, we left the Old World.'
Inscription on Columbus's caravels

'They are ill discoverers that think there is no land,
when they see nothing but sea.'
Sir Francis Bacon

'Do not fear risk. All exploration, all growth is calculated. Without
challenge people cannot reach their higher selves. Only if we are
willing to walk over the edge can we become winners.'
Anonymous

'Exploration is really the essence of the human spirit.'
Frank Borman

'The learn'd is happy nature to explore,
The fool is happy that knows no more.'
Alexander Pope

'He who has not travelled does not know the value of a man.'
Anonymous

'He travels fastest who travels alone.'
Rudyard Kipling

'Exploring is delightful to look forward to and back upon,
but it is not comfortable at the time, unless it be of such
an easy nature as not to deserve the name.'
Samuel Butler

> 'I seemed to vow to myself that some day I would go to the
> region of ice and snow and go on and on till I came to one of
> the poles of the Earth, the end of the axis upon which this
> great round ball turns.'
> **Sir Ernest Shackleton**

AROUND THE WORLD IN EIGHTY DAYS: CIRCUMNAVIGATORS

The Portuguese explorer Bartolomeu Diaz (c.1450–1500) was, in 1486, the first to sail round the Cape of Good Hope, which he called the Cape of Storms.

Vasco da Gama (1460–1524) was a Portuguese explorer who discovered an ocean route from Portugal to India – it was once believed that the Indian Ocean was not connected to any other seas.

John Cabot (1425–c.1500) was an Italian-born English explorer and navigator, who explored the Canadian coastline in search of the Northwest Passage – a seaway to Asia. Cabot actually thought he had reached Asia, but this was not to be.

In 1513, the Spanish explorer Vasco Núñez de Balboa (1475–1519) was the first European to see the eastern part of the Pacific Ocean, after crossing the Isthmus of Panama overland.

The Portuguese explorer Ferdinand Magellan (c.1480–1521) led the first expedition to circumnavigate the Earth after setting sail from Spain in 1519 with five ships and 270 men. He named the Pacific Ocean – 'pacific' meaning calm or peaceful – but the voyage was far from calm, for in 1521 Magellan was killed in a fight with the natives of Mactan Island in the Philippines, and never completed his round trip. In 1522, one of his ships, with only eighteen original crewmen, made it home.

The second around-the-world expedition was led by Sir Francis Drake (c.1540–96), a British admiral – as well as slave-trader and privateer. Though he set off with a fleet of five ships, four were lost to storms and fire, and on the lengthy voyage (from 1577 to 1580), only Drake was able to complete the journey in the *Golden Hind*.

Captain James Cook circumnavigated the globe at a high southern latitude, becoming the first European to cross the Antarctic Circle on 17 January 1773.

On 12 April 1961, the twenty-seven-year-old Soviet pilot Lt Yuri Gagarin (1934–68) circumnavigated the Earth in 108 minutes at an altitude of 327 km (203 miles) aboard the spacecraft *Vostock 1*.

Phineas Fogg, the fictional character in Jules Verne's celebrated 1873 novel, went *around* the world in eighty days.

The great explorer Sir Ernest Henry Shackleton died on South Georgia Island in 1922 during an attempt to circumnavigate the Antarctic continent.

In 1966, Sir Francis Chichester (1901–72) made a solo round-the-world trip in his yacht *Gypsy Moth*, with one stop on the way. It took him 226 days.

Dame Ellen MacArthur set a new record for sailing solo around the world in 2005: 71 days, 14 hours, 18 minutes and 33 seconds.

Mariners' Miscellany

- In ancient times, the seven seas were the Indian Ocean, the Black Sea, the Caspian Sea, the Adriatic Sea, the Persian Gulf, the Mediterranean Sea, and the Red Sea. Today we recognize more than fifty seas worldwide.

- The Greek philosopher Seleucus (of Seleucia; born *c*.190 BC) thought that the Moon was responsible for the tides. This notion would not be proved until the time of Isaac Newton, 1,800 years later.

- If it were possible to use the Northwest Passage, 5,000 nautical miles would be cut from shipping routes between Europe and Asia.

'There must be a beginning of any great matter, but the continuing unto the end until it be thoroughly finished yields the true glory.'
Sir Francis Drake

A BIT PEAKY: THE ASCENT OF MAN

MOUNTAIN	HEIGHT	FIRST CLIMBED BY	YEAR
Everest	8,850m	Edmund Hillary / Tenzing Norgay	1953
K2	8,611m	Lino Lacedelli / Achille Compagnoni	1954
Kilimanjaro	5,895m	Hans Meyer / Ludwig Purtscheller	1889
Mont Blanc	4,807m	Michel Paccard / Jaques Balmat	1786
Matterhorn	4,478m	Edward Whymper	1865
Ben Nevis	1,344m	James Robertson	1771
Snowdon	1,085m	Revs Peter Williams / W. Bingley	1798

CLIMB EVERY MOUNTAIN . . .

• Mount Everest is almost 9 km (5.5 miles) high. Named after Sir George Everest (1790–1866), a British military engineer who served as a Surveyor General of India from 1829 to 1843, Sir George became the first person to record the location and height of Mount Everest (which at that time was called Peak XV). Sir Andrew Walsh identified it as the tallest mountain in the world.

• Although a party of seven men led by the British climber and explorer Sir Edward Whymper (1840–1911) had been the first to reach the top of the Matterhorn, four of them – Charles Hudson, Francis Douglas, Douglas Hadow and Michel Croz – were killed during the descent.

• The world's second tallest mountain, K2, was first described by a British colonel, T. G. Montgomery, while he was surveying the area in 1856. He named the peaks in the order he saw them, K1, K2, K3, and so on. The K stands for Karakorum, the mountain range where K2 is found.

• The first person to climb Ben Nevis was eighteenth-century botanist James Robertson, while collecting plants for Edinburgh University.

• Mars has the largest mountain in the Solar System. Olympus Mons is 26 km (approx 16 miles) high – almost three times the height of Everest.

THOUGHTS ON TRAVEL

'Nobody climbs mountains for scientific reasons.
Science is used to raise money for the expeditions,
but you really climb for the hell of it.'
Edmund Hillary

'A journey of a thousand miles begins with a single step.'
Confucius

'They change their climate, not their soul, who rush across the sea.'
Horace

'The world is a book, and those who do not travel read only a page.'
St Augustine

'Two great talkers will not travel far together.'
Spanish proverb

'I love to travel, but hate to arrive.'
Albert Einstein

'Being in a ship is being in a jail, with the chance of being drowned.'
Samuel Johnson

'I have found out that there ain't no surer way to find out whether
you like people or hate them than to travel with them.'
Mark Twain

'Like all great travellers, I have seen more than I remember,
and remember more than I have seen.'
Benjamin Disraeli

'If you actually look like your passport photo,
you aren't well enough to travel.'
Sir Vivian Fuchs

'To travel hopefully is a better thing than to arrive,
and the true success is to labour.'
Robert Louis Stevenson

A (VERY) BRIEF HISTORY OF TIME

The appearance of a new Moon about every twenty-nine days was one way our early ancestors measured time. The first calendar was of a lunar variety, with the year comprising twelve moons.

Eventually it was realized that the Sun provided a more accurate measurement of time. Not only does it vary in height according to the time of day, but also according to the time of year. The first device used to measure time was a gnomon (essentially, a sundial) – a vertical stick or pillar that indicated the Sun's position by the length of its shadow. Obelisks and pyramids were also used for this purpose.

The ancient Chinese invented the ten Heavenly Stems and twelve Earthly Branches for chronological purposes. These signs are used to designate the hours, days, months and years. As most people were illiterate, animals were used to symbolize the Earthly Branches.

In about 300 BC, the Babylonian astronomer Berossus invented a sundial known as a hemicycle, which remained a popular tool for hundreds of years. Similarly, noted geometrists such as Ptolemy (c.AD 85–c.165) and Apollonius of Perga (third–second century BC) built complex sundials.

Around AD 900, the Arab astronomer Al-Battani (c.858–929) calculated the length of the year as 365 days, 5 hours, 48 minutes and 24 seconds. At that time, and for the next 600 years, Europe's calendar was based on a year of 365 days and 6 hours.

Mechanical clocks were invented in the fourteenth century.

Until about a hundred years ago, each city set its clocks to local time – noon was the time when the Sun was at its highest in the sky, as viewed from that city. So midday meals were served at different times in different cities.

The Earth is now divided into twenty-four time zones (each one a strip from North Pole to South Pole and about fifteen degrees of longitude wide) so that everyone in the world can be on roughly similar schedules.

In 1884, at an international conference in Washington, D.C., the world time zones were determined, each zone differing by one hour.

Heavy Dates

- According to an old English system of time units, a 'moment' is equal to one and a half minutes.

- Before Concorde was taken out of service, if you flew on it from London to New York, due to the time zones crossed, you could arrive two hours before you left.

- The entire world is on the same date only at the instant when it is noon in Greenwich, England, and midnight at the International Date Line.

- The wristwatch was invented in 1904 by Louis Cartier.

ABOUT TIME

'The long unmeasured pulse of time moves everything.
There is nothing hidden that it cannot bring to light,
nothing once known that may not become unknown.'
Sophocles

'Time is a great teacher, but unfortunately it kills all its pupils.'
Hector Berlioz

'I went to a restaurant that serves "breakfast at any time".
So I ordered French toast during the Renaissance.'
Steven Wright

'Put your hand on a hot stove for a minute, and it seems like an hour.
Sit with a pretty girl for an hour, and it seems like a minute.'
Albert Einstein's simple explanation of the theory of relativity

'As if you could kill time without injuring eternity.'
Henry David Thoreau

'Why kill time when one can employ it.'
French proverb

'Time wounds all heels.'
Groucho Marx

ADVENTURES IN TRANSPORTATION

Who's the craziest of them all? In 1824, Charles Blondin (1824–97) crossed Niagara Falls on a tightrope, almost 49 metres (160 feet) above the waterfall, and in 1901, sixty-four-year-old Annie Taylor became the first woman to go over these falls in a barrel.

On 15 September 1830, at the grand opening of the Manchester-to-Liverpool passenger railway line, William Huskisson, MP (1770–1830), inadvertently got in the way of Stephenson's 'Rocket', which badly mangled his leg. By dying from his injuries later that day, he became the first person to be killed by a train.

In 1863, London's Metropolitan Line opened and became the world's first underground railway.

In 1876, a law was passed that every ship had to have a line painted on its side. If the line sank below the water, the ship was deemed overloaded and was not allowed to sail. This line is still used today and is named after Samuel Plimsoll (1824–98), who made detailed studies of why so many ships sank.

Early bicycles were called 'boneshakers' before a Scottish vet, John Boyd Dunlop (1840–1921), introduced the pneumatic tyre in 1888.

The SOS signal was adopted as the international signal for distress in 1912. The first ship to use it was the *Titanic* in April of that year.

San Francisco's Golden Gate Bridge, completed in 1937, has enough steel wires in its cables to circle the Earth at the equator 3.5 times.

'Railway termini are our gates to the
glorious and the unknown. Through them
we pass out into adventure and sunshine;
to them, alas! we return.'
E. M. Forster

ACTS OF GOD III:
WINDS AND HURRICANES

In 1588, a major storm sank most of the Spanish Armada, killing an estimated 20,000 sailors.

In 1703, a catastrophic hurricane ripped across East Anglia. It was the worst storm in British history and killed perhaps as many as 15,000 people. During the storm, a ship at Whitstable in Kent was lifted from the sea and reputedly dropped some 229 metres (250 yards) inland, while Admiral Sir Cloudesley Shovell's flagship, *The Association*, was supposedly blown to Sweden. In London, Queen Anne sheltered in a cellar beneath St James's Palace.

The Great Hurricane of 1780 is thought to have been the most deadly of all times. It caused the deaths of 22,000 people across Martinique, St Lucia, St Vincent, St Kitts, Grenada and Barbados.

The great storm that struck southern England in October 1987 did a huge amount of damage, with 160-kph (100-mph) winds causing the deaths of eighteen people and the loss of 15 million trees. However, weatherman Michael Fish was correct: it was not a hurricane.

One of the first scales to estimate wind speeds was created by the British admiral Sir Francis Beaufort (1774–1856) in 1805. This was to help sailors estimate the winds via visual observations. The Beaufort Scale, which is still used today, starts with 0 and goes to a force of 12. Hurricane Force (Force 12) is classified as a wind of 64 knots (74 mph) or more, sustained over a period of at least ten minutes.

'God moves in a mysterious way
His wonders to perform;
He plants his footsteps in the sea,
And rides upon the storm.'
William Cowper

MUSICAL NOTES

> 'If thine enemy offend thee, give his child a drum.'
> **Anonymous**

Followers of sixth-century BC philosopher Pythagoras believed that the motions of the planets were mathematically related to musical sounds and numbers – 'The Music of the Spheres'.

The earliest known musical notation was used for the Vedic hymns of southern India around 700 BC.

When Pope Gregory I (*c.*540–604) wanted to write music down, he gave his notes (four in total) a corresponding letter – A to D – and soon monks were writing and singing Gregorian chants. We still use these notes today, with the later addition of E, F, G, and all the sharps and flats between each note on the scale.

The Benedictine monk Guido of Arezzo (995–1050) invented the music notations 'do, re, mi, fa, so, la, ti' (no, they didn't come from *The Sound of Music*) and drew them as notes on a staff.

Catastrophic Conducting

In 1687, the French composer Jean-Baptiste Lully died of a gangrenous abscess after piercing his foot with a baton while he was vigorously conducting a *Te Deum*.

> 'I understand the inventor of the bagpipes was inspired when he saw a man carrying an indignant, asthmatic pig under his arm. Unfortunately, the man-made sound never equalled the purity of the sound achieved by the pig.'
> **Alfred Hitchcock**

GREAT THINKERS I:
WISE WORDS OF PLATO

It is right to give every man his due.

Be kind, for everyone you meet is fighting a hard battle.

If women are expected to do the same work as men,
we must teach them the same things.

Ignorance – the root and the stem of every evil.

Man ... is a tame or civilized animal; nevertheless, he requires
proper instruction and a fortunate nature, and then of all animals he
becomes the most divine and most civilized; but if he be insufficiently
or ill-educated, he is the most savage of earthly creatures.

Never discourage anyone ... who continually makes progress,
no matter how slow.

No human thing is of serious importance.

The price good men pay for indifference to public affairs
is to be ruled by evil men.

You can discover more about a person in an hour of play
than in a year of conversation.

Necessity, who is the mother of invention.

The beginning is the most important part of the work.

He was a wise man who invented beer.

Death is not the worst that can happen to men.

Wise men talk because they have something to say;
fools, because they have to say something.

WISE GUYS III

'No airship will ever fly from New York to Paris.
That seems to me impossible.'
Wilbur Wright (the co-inventor of the aeroplane), in 1909

'The popular mind often pictures gigantic flying machines speeding
across the Atlantic carrying innumerable passengers in a way
analogous to our modern steamships. It seems safe to say that
such ideas are wholly visionary.'
Astronomer William H. Pickering in 1910

'Young man, I am afraid you are wasting your time. If there were any
more planets they would have been found long before this.'
**Visiting astronomer to Clyde Tombaugh, before he
discovered Pluto in 1930**

'There is not the slightest indication that nuclear energy will
ever be obtainable. It would mean that the atom would have
to be shattered at will.'
Albert Einstein in 1932

'The bomb will never go off. I speak as an expert in explosives.'
Admiral William Leahy, US Atomic Bomb Project

'Housewives in fifty years may wash dirty dishes right down the drain.
Cheap plastic will melt in hot water.'
Popular Mechanics, **1950**

'Nuclear-powered vacuum cleaners will be a reality within ten years.'
New York Times, **1955**

'Space travel is utter bilge.'
**Sir Richard van der Riet Woolley, UK Astronomer Royal,
a year before *Sputnik* in 1956**

ACTS OF GOD IV: VOLCANOES

In 1500 BC, the island of Thera in the Mediterranean island group of Santorini literally blew up. The explosion, and the tsunami which followed, virtually wiped out the Minoan civilization in the area.

In AD 79, about 3,360 people died, including Pliny the Elder, in the eruption of Vesuvius, near Naples, which destroyed the cities of Pompeii and Herculaneum. Vesuvius had also erupted in 5960 BC and 3580 BC, producing the largest known eruptions in Europe. In 1631, mud and lava flows from the volcano killed another 3,500 people. It remains active to this day.

In 1707, Mount Fuji in Japan erupted for the last time (to date).

On 26 August 1883, Krakatau (Krakatoa) in Indonesia exploded with the force of 100,000 hydrogen bombs. Fine ashes from the eruption were carried by upper-level winds as far away as New York City, the explosion was heard more than 3,000 miles away, fine pumice covered the sea for hundreds of miles, and volcanic dust blew into the upper atmosphere affecting the Earth's weather, and giving red sunrises and sunsets for five years. Tsunamis up to 40 metres (131 feet) high were generated by the explosion. Approximately 36,000 people died.

In 1980, Mount St Helens in the state of Washington, USA, exploded with an energy equivalent to 10 million tons of TNT.

Scientists have discovered that the ground in Yellowstone National Park is 74 cm (29 inches) higher than it was in 1923 for the simple reason that the whole area is a supervolcano which is overdue for eruption. The last supervolcano to erupt was Toba, in Sumatra, 74,000 years ago. The eruption caused the obliteration of the Sun's rays, a nuclear winter and the failure of most plant life. Mankind, too, was nearly annihilated . . .

> 'It is more important to know what sort of person has a disease
> than to know what sort of disease a person has.'
> **Hippocrates**

MATTERS MEDICAL I:
EARLY DIAGNOSIS

Acupuncture was first used as a medical treatment in 2,700 BC by the
Chinese Emperor Shen Nung (ruled 2737–2697 BC).

Hippocrates of Cos (460–370 BC) is credited as being the 'father of
medicine'. He and his followers compiled a body of literature on
medical practice known as the *Corpus Hippocraticum*, which consists
of some seventy books (although it is unknown whether Hippocrates
actually wrote any of them). They also created the Hippocratic Oath,
a code of conduct for physicians.

Herophilus of Chalcedon (*c.*335–*c.*280 BC) and Erasistratus of Ceos
(325–250 BC) were two of the first anatomists. They performed public
dissections, sometimes on prisoners who were still alive. Needless to
say, they made a lot of discoveries about the inner workings of the
human body: the former made studies of the brain, spleen, liver, sexual
organs and nervous system, while the latter is said to have been the
first to trace arteries and veins to the heart.

The Roman scholar and writer Marcus Terentius Varro (116–27 BC)
thought that disease was caused by tiny living things that were too
small to see. However, even after the microscope was invented in 1609,
scientists couldn't accept this.

Aulus Cornelius Celsus was a first-century Roman encyclopædist
whose *De Medicina*, believed to have been written about AD 30, was
rediscovered in 1478. The work contains descriptions of several
operations, including tonsillectomies and early excision of lumps in
the breast.

The most famous doctor in the Roman Empire was a Greek named
Claudius Galen (AD *c.*129–*c.*216). Physician to Marcus Aurelius,
Commodius and Septimius Severus, Galen proved that urine was
formed in the kidneys, correctly identified seven of the twelve cranial

nerves, discovered the valves of the heart, recognized the contagiousness of tuberculosis, and of rabies via dogs, and discovered that arteries carry blood.

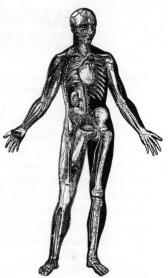

The Greek physician Paul of Aegina (625–690) wrote of such operations as tracheotomy, tonsillectomy, bronchotomy, staphylotomy, and the removal of the breast as a cure for cancer.

Avicenna (980–1037) was a Persian physician, philosopher and scientist, considered by many to be 'the father of modern medicine'. His most famous works are *The Book of Healing* and *The Canon of Medicine*.

GREAT THINKERS II: WISE WORDS OF MARCUS AURELIUS

Because a thing seems difficult for you, do not think it impossible for anyone to accomplish.

Do every act of your life as if it were your last.

Everything we hear is an opinion, not a fact. Everything we see is a perspective, not the truth.

If it is not right, do not do it; if it is not true, do not say it.

Poverty is the mother of crime.

That which is not good for the beehive cannot be good for the bees.

The art of living is more like wrestling than dancing.

There are three classes into which all the women past seventy that ever I knew were to be divided:
1. That dear old soul; 2. That old woman; 3. That old witch.

MATTERS MEDICAL II:
SOME DEADLY DISEASES

Smallpox has been responsible for the deaths of millions throughout the world. In the twentieth century alone there were an estimated 300–500 million smallpox victims. Whole civilizations in the Americas were wiped out by the disease – sometimes deliberately. In China, Turkey and India, people tried to defeat smallpox by purposely introducing the live virus to a wound. There was a one in four chance of developing the full-blown disease, but others just got a mild version of it and became immune. Then, on 14 May 1796, British physician Edward Jenner (1749–1823) tried out his first inoculation against smallpox by using a vaccine containing cowpox fluid, followed by a smallpox vaccine two months later. It worked. In 1979, the World Health Organization declared the eradication of smallpox.

Anthrax – a disease of animals and humans that causes sores on the lungs – has been around a long time. In fact the fifth and sixth plagues in the book of Exodus may have been outbreaks of anthrax, as may the 'Black Bane', which swept through Europe in the seventeenth century. In 1876, the German doctor Robert Koch devised a procedure to demonstrate that the bacterium *Bacillus anthracis* causes anthrax. Five years later, in 1881, anthrax became the first bacterial disease for which immunization was available.

Leprosy is one of the world's oldest known diseases, and can be traced to ancient China, Egypt and India. It was also rampant in Europe during the thirteenth century. Leprosy is one of the most stigmatized diseases – sufferers were banished to 'leper colonies' – but it is now curable with multi-drug therapy. Since 1985 over 12 million people have been cured of the disease.

The worldwide **'Spanish Flu'** epidemic that broke out in 1918 killed more than 30 million people in less than a year. In the US, physicians put the blame on nakedness, fish contaminated by Germans, dirt, dust, unclean pyjamas, Chinese people, open windows, closed windows, old books, and cosmic influences. In reality the virus started in pigs.

Rabies sufferers were originally all doomed to die a horrible death. At one time, those bitten by an infected animal would have their wounds burned with a red-hot iron, or perhaps have had limbs amputated, but all to no avail. However, in 1885, the French scientist Louis Pasteur (1822–95) was working on a vaccination derived from rabbits that had died of rabies. When a young boy called Joseph Meister (c.1876–1940), was brought to his laboratory close to death, having been bitten all over by a rabid dog, Pasteur used his vaccine for the first time and found it to be a success.

Diphtheria gets its name from the Greek word *dipthera* meaning skin or hide. It was coined in 1855 by the French physician Armand Trousseau (1801–67) with reference to the leather-like membrane that grows on the tonsils, throat and in the nose of a victim, obstructing the airways. Diphtheria was once a dreaded disease, children being particularly vulnerable to it. Through the 1920s it struck about 150,000 people a year, and killed about 15,000 of them. One of the first effective treatments was discovered in the 1880s by US physician Joseph O'Dwyer (1841–98), who developed tubes that could be inserted into the throat to prevent victims from suffocating. In the 1890s, the German physician Emil von Behring (1854–1917) developed an anti-toxin which, although it did not kill the bacteria, neutralized the toxic poisons that the bacteria released into the body.

Polio, or poliomyelitis, crippled thousands of children during a worldwide epidemic in the 1940s and 1950s. It is estimated that one of every 5,000 people (mostly children) fell victim to polio. Some were totally paralysed and needed to live in 'iron lungs' to breathe. The epidemic was ended by Jonas Salk (1914–95), a research physician who formulated a vaccine against the devastating disease.

Tuberculosis (TB) is caused by the bacterium *Mycobacterium tuberculosis*. It is a disease with a long history as skeletal remains from 6,000-year-old humans have been revealed to show signs of TB. Known as 'consumption', from the way in which a sufferer's body seemed to be consumed by its symptoms, it is believed that during the Great Plague and Great Fire, in the mid 1660s, one out of every five London citizens had TB. Robert Koch discovered the tubercle bacillus in 1882, which led to the development of a vaccine for its prevention.

SOME EPONYMOUS DISEASES

DISEASE	NAMED AFTER
Addison's disease	Thomas Addison (1793–1860)
Alzheimer's disease	Alois Alzheimer (1864–1915)
Asperger's syndrome	Hans Asperger (1906–80)
Cock peculiar tumour	Edward Cock (1805–92)
Down's syndrome	John Langdon-Down (1828–96)
Goodpasture's syndrome	Ernest Goodpasture (1886–1960)
Hodgkin's disease	Thomas Hodgkin (1798–1866)
Huntington's disease	George Huntington (1850–1916)
Paget's disease	James Paget (1814–99)
Parkinson's disease	James Parkinson (1755–1824)
Pott's disease	Percivall Pott (1714–88)
Raynaud's disease	Maurice Raynaud (1834–81)
Tourette's syndrome	Gilles de la Tourette (1857–1904)

PAIN, PAIN, GO AWAY . . .

Around 2,000 years ago, there was a worldwide belief that pain existed outside the body and entered it as an actual force. It was thought to be a punishment from the gods, and so some people held the view that it should be endured. Others who weren't quite so stoical – or stupid – came up with the alternative of pain relief.

A container full of marijuana was discovered in the 2,000-year-old grave of a Scythian princess.

Around 1550 BC, patients were advised to drink a mixture of yeast, juniper and beer for four days to cure pain.

The ancient Egyptians used over 500 plants, wild and cultivated, for medicinal purposes.

Willow bark provides the salicylic acid from which aspirin was originally synthesized. It was used as a pain remedy by the Greeks 2,500 years ago.

The sleeping sponge, a sea sponge that was saturated with the mixed juices of soporific plants, was used to prevent pain during surgery.

In 1543, the French surgeon Ambroise Paré (1510–90) promoted the practice of anaesthesia by applying pressure to the nerves. He also used a technique to minimize pain for the dressing of wounds by applying a salve of egg yolks, oil of roses and turpentine to the sore.

Ether was discovered in the sixteenth century by Valerius Cordus (1515–44), who called it 'sweet vitriol', although it wasn't used for anaesthetic purposes for another 300 years.

Queen Victoria (1819–1901) used marijuana to ease the discomfort of menstrual cramps.

Louis Pasteur (1822–95) wrote in his laboratory notes, 'This damned mould keeps destroying my cultures.' It was the 'damned mould' that gave us penicillin.

Anaesthesia was first induced successfully in 1846 by the US dental surgeon William Morton (1819–68), who used ether for the first time on a patient before a difficult tooth extraction. Chloroform was introduced in 1847, and nitrogen protoxide in 1868.

Morphine, an alkaloid derived from opium, was named after Morpheus, the Greek god of dreams, by the German pharmacist Friedrich Sertürner (d.1841).

Opium, ginseng, Siberian wort, willow, mandrake, hemlock, leaves of *Erythroxylon coca* (cocaine), mandragora, rhubarb, snow, ice, whisky, gin, rum, morphine, hashish, laughing gas, mesmerism are just a few things that have been tried as pain relief.

UNUSUAL DEMISES

> 'Woe is me. I think I am becoming a god.'
> **Emperor Vespasian, when fatally ill**

In 456 BC, the Greek dramatist Aeschylus (525–456 BC) died when a vulture dropped a tortoise on his head from a great height.

In 453, Attila the Hun (c.406–453) suffered a severe nosebleed on his wedding night and choked to death.

In 964, Pope John XII (c.937–964) was beaten to death by the husband of a woman with whom he was having an affair.

In 1277, Pope John XXI (1215–77) was killed when his scientific laboratory collapsed.

In 1559, Henry II of France (1519–59) died after being accidentally hit on the head with a lance by one of his Scots Guards.

In 1601, the Danish astronomer Tycho Brahe (1546–1601) died after his bladder burst during a banquet.

In 1841, William Henry Harrison (1773–1841), ninth President of the United States, gave the longest inaugural address in the history of America in heavy snow and caught a cold. It developed into pneumonia and he was dead within a month.

In 1869, John Augustus Roebling (1806–69) – designer of the Brooklyn Bridge in New York – died of a tetanus infection after having his leg crushed by a ferryboat while working on the bridge.

In 1911, Jack Daniel (c.1850–1911), founder of the famous Tennessee whiskey distillery, died of blood poisoning following a toe injury he received after kicking his safe when he forgot the combination code.

In 1920, Alexander I of Greece (1893–1920) died from blood poisoning after being bitten by his gardener's pet monkey.

In 1923, the jockey Frank Hayes suffered a heart attack during a horse race. The horse went on to finish first, making Hayes the only deceased jockey to win a race.

Death By Ballet

Wilhelm II of Germany (1859–1941), known to the British as Kaiser Bill, was prone to extreme fits of immense anger. Once when he arrived unexpectedly at one of his army bases, the men were unprepared and had no entertainment available. Wilhelm was so enraged that he forced one of his highest-ranking generals, Dietrich von Hülsen-Haeseler, chief of the military cabinet, to put on a tutu and perform some ballet. The general, who was extremely unfit and overweight, promptly keeled over and died.

GREAT THINKERS III:
WISE WORDS OF ARISTOTLE

Personal beauty is a greater recommendation than
any letter of reference.

A flatterer is a friend who is your inferior, or pretends to be so.

Change in all things is sweet.

The appropriate age for marriage is around eighteen for girls
and thirty-seven for men.

It is unbecoming for young men to utter maxims.

Mothers are fonder than fathers of their children because
they are more certain they are their own.

Pleasure in the job puts perfection in the work.

The gods too are fond of a joke.

In nine cases out of ten, a woman had better show
more affection than she feels.

If one way be better than another, that you may be
sure is nature's way.

EARLY DAUBS

> 'God is really only another artist. He invented the giraffe,
> the elephant, and the cat. He has no real style. He just
> goes on trying other things.'
> **Pablo Picasso**

The earliest cave paintings were made using iron oxides.

The ancient Egyptians developed paints from pigments in the soil (yellow, orange, and red). On a bizarre note, they also ground up mummies to make a paint known as 'mummy brown'.

One of the earliest colour discoveries was made by Plato, who found that by mixing two colours, a third is produced.

The Romans gave us the colour purple. To obtain a pound of royal purple dye, 4 million molluscs had to be crushed.

The Aztecs came up with crimson red, which they produced by crushing millions of cochineal beetles.

Indian yellow was made by mixing concentrated cattle urine with mud.

By 1880, it was possible to buy paints in tins, in a wide range of colours.

The first spray paint was invented by Edward H. Seymour in 1949.

No Olive Oils

The Dutch painter Piet Mondrian (1872–1944) never used green in his works.

> '"I know of only two painters in the world," said a newly introduced
> feminine enthusiast to Whistler, "yourself and Velásquez."
> "Why," answered Whistler in dulcet tones, "why drag in Velásquez?"'
> **D. C. Seitz, of James McNeill Whistler**

BROAD BRUSHSTROKES

Leonardo da Vinci (1452–1519) spent twelve years painting the Mona Lisa's lips. A recent explanation of her enigmatic smile has concluded that she is not smiling at all; rather her expression is one common to people who have lost their front teeth.

Italian painter Caravaggio (1571–1610) fled Rome in 1606 after killing a young man in a duel.

Dutch painter Rembrandt (1606–69) painted over sixty self-portraits.

Artist and writer Edward Lear (1812–88) loved his pet cat so much that when he moved to Italy he had a replica of his former home built so that the cat wouldn't feel disorientated.

When Auguste Rodin (1840–1917) exhibited *The Bronze Period* in 1878, critics thought he had cheated by taking a plaster cast of a model.

In the last decade of his life Claude Monet (1840–1926) painted a group of large water lily murals (*Nymphéas*) for the Musée de l'Orangerie in Paris, by which time he was nearly blind.

Vincent van Gogh (1853–90) sold only one painting while he was alive – *Red Vineyard at Arles*.

In 1961, the painting *Le Bateau*, by Henri Matisse (1869–1954), was exhibited upside-down at the Museum of Modern Art in New York. It hung there for forty-six days before anyone noticed.

Pablo Picasso (1881–1973) completed twenty-three of his major paintings in one month.

THE SECRET OF LIFE

By the Second World War, researchers knew that it was DNA, or deoxyribonucleic acid, that contained billions of units of genetic information and carried our genes from one generation to the next. However, until the 1950s no one had any idea how it worked or what it looked like. Then, on 28 February 1953, Francis Crick (1916–2004) announced that he had found the secret of life. He and his collaborator James Watson (b. 1928) had identified the double-helix structure of DNA – a discovery that would be the basis for many of the achievements of biology, medicine and forensics thereafter.

Gene Pools

- The Austrian monk Gregor Mendel (1822–84) deduced the basic rules of heredity from studying garden peas. Although he did not receive great recognition in his lifetime, he is now regarded as the father of the study of genetics.

- The word 'gene' was first used in 1909, in a book by the Danish geneticist Wilhelm Ludvig Johannsen (1857–1927).

SCIENTIFIC DEFINITIONS

If it moves, it's biology
If it stinks, it's chemistry
If it doesn't work, it's physics
If it doesn't apply, it's economics
If it keeps up, man will atrophy all his limbs
but the push-button finger.
Frank Lloyd Wright

If it's green, it's biology
If it stinks, it's chemistry
If it has numbers it's math
If it doesn't work, it's technology.
Anonymous

A WORD ON INVENTIONS

'To invent, you need a good imagination and a pile of junk.'
Thomas Edison

'A person with a new idea is a crank until the idea succeeds.'
Mark Twain

'An inventor is a person who makes an ingenious arrangement
of wheels, levers and springs, and believes it civilization.'
Ambrose Bierce

'Results! Why man, I have gotten a lot of results.
I know several thousand things that won't work.'
Thomas Edison

AN A–Z OF INVENTIONS

ADHESIVE TAPE
Invented by Richard G. Drew (1899–1980), an engineer for the
Minnesota Mining company. He developed masking tape by 1925
and Scotch tape five years later.

BIRO
Invented in 1935 by Hungarian László Biró (1899–1985). Although
John Loud, an American leather tanner, had invented a ballpoint
marker much earlier (in 1888), sadly for him, his pen leaked.

CONTACT LENSES
A type of contact lens was envisioned by Leonardo da Vinci as
early as the sixteenth century, but they were properly invented in
1887 by the German physiologist Adolf Eugen Fick (1829–1901),
who apparently made them first for animals.

DYNAMO
Having invented the electric motor in 1821, chemist and physicist
Michael Faraday (1791–1867) went on to invent the dynamo and
the transformer in 1831.

ELEVATOR BRAKE

Fancy going in a lift without one? Elisha Graves Otis (1811–61) invented the elevator brake using a ratchet on a spring to catch the lift in the event of an accident. It was also thanks to Otis that the skyscraper was made possible – a mixed blessing, perhaps?

FIRE EXTINGUISHER

In 1813, George William Manby (1765–1854) watched firemen struggling to put out a fire in a building in Edinburgh. He noticed that the men couldn't get their hoses to the higher floors quickly enough. Thus he invented a portable extinguisher.

GAS MASKS

When the Germans started to use gas as a weapon in the First World War, the British Army sent its soldiers back into action with a piece of chemically treated cloth fixed over their mouths and noses. The first true gas masks were called respirators.

HOVERCRAFT

On 11 June 1959, the over-water craft SRN-I, or 'hovercraft', was viewed by the press. Its inventor was Sir Christopher Cockerell (1910–99).

INVISIBLE INK

There are various invisible 'inks' – for example, rice water becomes visible when iodine is added to it. During the Indian Mutiny of 1857–8, the British wrote secret messages in a solution of milk and lemon juice; they became visible if the writing was exposed to heat.

JEANS

Levi Strauss (1829–1902) was a one-time tailor in Buttenheim, Bavaria. Strauss emigrated to America with his family in 1847, where he made a living selling dry goods, including tents and linens to the 49ers (the people who came to the California Gold Rush, which began in earnest in 1849). In 1873, Strauss and Jacob Davis, a Nevada tailor, patented Davis's idea of using copper rivets at the stress points of sturdy work trousers. Early Levi's, called 'waist overalls', came in a brown canvas duck fabric and a heavy blue denim fabric. The duck-fabric pants were not a great success, and were dropped early on, but the popularity of the blue denims made Strauss's business extremely profitable.

KHAKI

This was first used in India in 1848, by the Corps of Guides under the command of Sir Harry Lumsden (1821–96). The name comes from the Urdu word *khak* meaning dust. The dust-coloured uniforms became popular; not only did they camouflage the dirt, but they also made their wearers less visible targets.

LEAD PENCIL

The 'lead' pencil was invented in 1564, and actually contained no lead at all. In fact it used graphite in the middle – which was then known as black lead.

MICROWAVE OVEN

The microwave oven was invented as an accidental by-product of 1940s wartime radar research using magnetrons (vacuum tubes that produce microwave radiation). In 1946, a Raytheon Corporation engineer, Dr Percy LeBaron Spencer (1894–1970), was working on magnetrons. One day he noticed a chocolate bar in his pocket had melted, which he realized had been caused by the microwaves he was working with. After experimenting, he realized that microwaves would cook foods quickly – even faster than conventional ovens that cook with heat. In 1954, the Raytheon Corporation produced the first commercial microwave oven – the 1161 Radarange.

NON-STICK PAN

In 1938, Dr Roy Plunkett (1910–94) discovered polytetrafluorethylene. It was later stuck on to frying pans in the 1950s, so that eggs and bacon didn't.

ORGAN TRANSPLANT

In 1957, Willem Kolff (b.1911), who devised the kidney dialysis machine in 1945, implanted an artificial heart into a dog for the first time. The dog survived for ninety minutes. In the early 1960s, Christiaan Barnard began experimenting with heart transplantation. His first patient survived the operation, but died eighteen days later from a lung infection.

PAPER CLIP

The paper clip was invented in the late nineteenth century by a Norwegian patent clerk called Johann Vaaler. His original paper clip was a thin spring-steel wire with triangular or square ends and two 'tongues'. Vaaler patented his invention in Germany and later in the USA (1901). The modern-shaped paper clip was patented in 27 April 1899 by William Middlebrook of Waterbury, Connecticut, USA.

QUININE
In 1742, the Countess of Cinchona was believed to have discovered that the bark of the South American cinchona tree has anti-malarial properties when native healers cured her of the disease with it. However, it was not until the 1850s that this knowledge really caught on with Europeans, after the French researchers Pierre-Joseph Pelletier (1788–1842) and Joseph Caventou (1795–1877) extracted, isolated and named quinine in 1820. The name derives from the South American Indian word for the cinchona tree bark. British colonials in India found the quinine tonic bitter tasting, so they mixed it with gin, and thus gin and tonic was born.

RUBBER BAND
The first rubber band was made in 1845 by Stephen Perry of the rubber manufacturing company Messrs Perry and Co., in London, England. Perry invented the rubber band, which was made of vulcanized rubber, to hold papers or envelopes together.

SAFETY PIN
The modern safety pin was invented by Walter Hunt in 1849 – to pay off a debt of fifteen dollars – though early safety pins have been around since the Bronze Age.

TEA BAG
Tea bags were invented by Thomas Sullivan in 1908. The first bags were made from silk as a way of packaging an individual sample of tea, but people opted to brew it up, silk and all.

UMBRELLA
The English inventor Samuel Fox (1815–87) invented and manufactured the steel-ribbed umbrella in 1852. (Rain-protecting devices made of wood or whalebone had been used before.)

VACUUM CLEANER
In 1901, Hubert Booth lay on the floor, put his handkerchief over his mouth, and sucked. When he removed the handkerchief, he observed that dirt had been trapped in it, drawn in by his sucking. His first vacuum cleaner, which was horse-drawn, was parked outside the house, and the dirt from inside was sucked up by an 800-foot hose. However, due to the loud noise

it made while sucking up the dirt, Booth found himself in trouble with the police on occasions. Fortunately, vacuum-cleaner designs have got a little more compact and less noisy since.

WORLD WIDE WEB
Tim Berners-Lee invented the World Wide Web. His first version was a program named 'Enquire' (Enquire Within Upon Everything), which he developed while working at CERN, the European Particle Physics Laboratory in Geneva, Switzerland. He invented the system as a way of sharing scientific data (and other information) around the world, using the Internet, a global network of computers, and hypertext documents. He devised HTML (HyperText Mark-up Language), the basic language for the Web, and created URLs (Universal Resource Locators) to designate the location of each web page. HTTP (HyperText Transfer Protocol) was his set of rules for linking to pages on the Web. In 1990 he wrote the first browser to set the World Wide Web in motion. Its growth was (and still is) phenomenal, and has made information more accessible than ever before.

X-RAYS
These electromagnetic rays were discovered in 1895 by German physicist Wilhelm Konrad von Röntgen (1845–1923). He created this new form of radiation to allow him to photograph objects that were hidden behind opaque shields, and even photographed part of his own skeleton. X-rays were soon used as an important diagnostic tool in medicine. Röntgen called these waves 'X-radiation' because so little was known about them.

YALE LOCK
This was invented by the American lock manufacturer Linus Yale (1821–68) and came into use in the 1860s. Practically no two Yale keys are identical, except the ones held by people using the same front door, of course.

ZIP
The zip or zipper was invented in 1890 by Whitcomb L. Judson (1836–1909), a Chicago engineer. Despite his efforts, he wasn't able to convince people of its potential, and he died without ever seeing his fastener on a pair of jeans.

ROADWORTHY MILESTONES

The world's first traffic offender was French army captain N. J. Cugnot. Having built a steam-powered mechanical tractor to pull cannon in 1709, he crashed it and was thrown in jail.

The first traffic lights (powered by gas lamps) were installed outside the Houses of Parliament in 1868. Unfortunately they blew up and killed a policeman.

Number plates were used for the first time on Parisian cars in 1893. Ten years later car registration was introduced to Britain.

In Britain, only the Queen is allowed to drive around without number plates, which makes her car rather easy to spot . . .

The first speed camera was tried out in Paris in 1900 and the first speed humps in Illinois in 1907.

The first roadside petrol pump in Britain was installed in 1920.

In 1924, the first motorway was built in Italy. It covered a distance of 85 km (53 miles), from Milan to Varese.

The world's first compulsory driving test was imposed on a Mr Bean in 1935.

A 30-mph speed limit was imposed in British towns in 1935, and yet speedometers didn't appear in cars until 1937.

There were a million cars on British roads by 1932.

Sir Malcolm Campbell (1885–1948), the renowned land-speed racer, was once stopped by the police for speeding on a bicycle.

The first parking meters were installed in Oklahoma City in 1935. Britain did not have them until 1958, when 625 meters were set up across London.

Dr Jacques Locard of France invented the breathalyser in 1952, but he died before patenting it.

In 1960, the Morris Minor became the first car to sell a million in Britain.

One of the biggest traffic jams ever was caused in January 1990 when thousands of East Germans packed up their worldly goods and drove to West Germany.

GREAT THINKERS IV:
WISE WORDS OF SOCRATES

By all means marry. If you get a good wife, you'll be happy;
if you get a bad one, you'll become a philosopher.

Beware the barrenness of a busy life.

The greatest way to live with honour in this world is
to be what we pretend to be.

Do not do to others what angers you if done to you by others.

Envy is the ulcer of the soul.

Think not those faithful who praise all thy words and actions;
but those who kindly reprove thy faults.

Thou shouldst eat to live; not live to eat.

Wind buffs up empty bladders; opinion, fools.

The unexamined life is not worth living.

UP, UP AND AWAY:
THE BUSINESS OF FLYING

The kite was the first man-made aircraft. It was invented in China as
early as 1000 BC, but does not seem to have appeared in Europe until
the fourteenth century.

There were man-lifting kites in the Orient, but it was not until 1893,
when Lawrence Hargrave (1850–1915) invented the stable box kite,
that Europeans fancied being lifted by kite.

Robert Baden-Powell (1857–1941) experimented with being flown by
kite in 1894, and in 1904 S. F. Cody's man-lifting kite was used by the
British for naval and military observation.

The Marquis d'Arlandes and Pilâtre
de Rozier (1754–85) were the first
people to make a true hot-air-
balloon flight when, on 21
November 1783, they managed to
stay airborne for twenty minutes
over Paris. Pilâtre de Rozier was
later killed in an attempt to cross
the Channel in a balloon.

In the mid-1800s it took fifteen days to cross the Atlantic by
steamship; in the 1920s the hydrogen airship *Graf Zeppelin* took
just two days. However, on 7 May 1937, the airship *Hindenburg* –
the largest rigid airship ever built – caught fire as she docked at
Lakehurst, New Jersey, killing thirty-six of the ninety-seven
passengers. Unsurprisingly, people weren't too keen on that form
of travel after the disaster.

Leonardo da Vinci produced sketches of a helicopter-like machine
400 years before a real one appeared in 1907.

The first powered aeroplane to fly properly was invented by Wilbur and Orville Wright (respectively 1867–1912 and 1871–1948). Their 'Wright Flyer' was a fabric-covered biplane with a wooden frame, powered by a 12-horsepower water-cooled engine. On 17 December 1903, the brothers flew their plane at Kitty Hawk in North Carolina. The flight lasted for twelve seconds, and covered a distance of 36.5 metres (120 feet).

The first Atlantic crossing by air was on 27 May 1919. After setting off from Newfoundland and landing in Lisbon, Portugal, Lieutenant Commander Albert Read radioed to say: 'We are safely on the other side of the pond.' It was not a non-stop flight, however.

In 1919, Captain John Alcock (1892–1919) and Lieutenant Arthur Whitten-Brown (1896–1948), both British pilots, flew non-stop across the Atlantic – and landed in an Irish bog.

Charles Lindbergh (1902–74) was the first person to fly solo non-stop across the Atlantic in 1927.

The supersonic Concorde jet made its first trial flight on 1 January 1969.

WHY DID THE CHICKEN CROSS THE ROAD?

Aristotle: It is the nature of chickens to cross roads.

Isaac Newton: Chickens at rest tend to stay at rest; chickens in motion tend to cross roads.

Albert Einstein: Whether the chicken crossed the road or the road moved beneath the chicken depends on your frame of reference.

Werner Heisenberg: We are not sure which side of the road the chicken was on, but it was moving very fast.

Wolfgang Pauli: There already was a chicken on this side of the road.

August Mobius: To get to the same side.

IT'S A LONG WAY DOWN

The ancient Chinese made reference to parachute jumps, using hats
and umbrellas. Leonardo da Vinci designed a parachute in 1485.
However, the first official parachute jump was the one made by
André-Jacques Garnerin (1759–1823) in 1797. He was dropped from a
balloon about 6,500 feet over the Parc Monceau in Paris. His chute
was made of white canvas with a basket attached. His descent was
fast and unsteady, and Garnerin was violently sick as he descended.
However, his chute served him well and got him to terra firma safely.

An inspiration to the Wright Brothers, flight pioneer Otto Lilienthal
(1849–96) built, flew and killed himself flying gliders in the 1890s.

Thomas Selfridge (1882–1908) was the first man to die in a powered-
aeroplane accident on 17 September 1908. He was a passenger in a US
War Department test plane flown by Wilbur Wright, which crashed.

On 12 July 1910, Charles Rolls (1877–1910), co-founder of Rolls-Royce,
became the first person to die in an air crash in the UK. He was in a
Wright Brothers' biplane, which came down in a Bournemouth field.

FAMOUS AIR-CRASH VICTIMS

Amelia Earhart – 2 July 1937
Amy Johnson – 5 January 1941
Carole Lombard – 16 January 1942
Glenn Miller – 14 December 1944
The Busby Babes – 6 February 1958
Buddy Holly – 3 February 1959
Patsy Cline, Hawkshaw Hawkins, Cowboy Copas – 5 March 1963
Otis Redding – 10 December 1967
Alexander Onassis – 22 January 1973
John F. Kennedy, Jnr – 16 July 1999

ACTS OF GOD V:
WHERE THERE'S SMOKE

> ' . . . there hapned to break out, a sad and deplorable
> Fire in Pudding-lane . . . This lamentable Fire in a short
> time became too big to be mastred by any Engines . . .'
> ***London Gazette*, 1666**

In AD 64, a fire left much of Rome in ruins. Some citizens suspected that the Emperor Nero started the fire himself, to make way for the building of an extravagant palace, but this wasn't so, as he was out of the city at the time the fire began.

On 2 September 1666, Thomas Farynor, a Pudding Lane baker, forgot to check his oven before going to bed. As he slept, sparks flew out of it which set fire to a pile of wood and then his house. The summer had been a dry one and a warm east wind soon blew the fire on to his neighbour's house, and the next. By Thursday 6 September, when the fire died out, four-fifths of the City of London had burnt down. A total of 13,000 houses were lost, 18 churches, London Bridge and St Paul's Cathedral. Only six people were killed, although thousands were left homeless.

In 1894, Minnesota's Hinckley fire destroyed twelve towns, leaving 450 people dead and 160,000 acres devastated.

In 1906, fires following an earthquake in San Francisco destroyed the city, leaving 500 people dead or missing and 28,188 buildings destroyed. The flames were so intense that silver coins in the banks fused into ingots.

In 1910, a 'Great Fire' destroyed 3 million acres in Idaho and Montana, leaving 86 people dead.

In 1970, the Cairo Opera House was destroyed by fire. Unfortunately, the city's fire station was located inside the same building.

> 'People who fight fire with fire usually end up with ashes.'
> **Abigail van Buren**

SOME LAWS OF SCIENCE TO BEAR IN MIND

Enough research will tend to support your theory.

An object in motion will be heading in the wrong direction.

An object at rest will be in the wrong place.

If an experiment works, something has gone wrong.

No matter what the anticipated result, there will always be someone eager (a) to misinterpret it, (b) to fake it, or (c) to believe it happened according to his own pet theory.

In any collection of data, the figure most obviously correct, beyond all need of checking, is the mistake.

The chance of the bread falling with the butter side down is directly proportional to the value of the carpet.

Anyone who makes a significant contribution to any field of endeavour, and stays in that field long enough, becomes an obstruction to its progress – in direct proportion to the importance of their original contribution.

If an elderly but distinguished scientist says that something is possible he is almost certainly right, but if he says that it is impossible he is very probably wrong.

THE CONFUSION OF ALBERT EINSTEIN

Albert Einstein (1879–1955) was a German theoretical physicist who is widely regarded as the greatest scientist of the twentieth century. He proposed the theory of relativity and also played a significant role in the development of quantum mechanics, statistical mechanics, and cosmology. In 1905 he submitted a series of papers which included the famous equation that the energy of a body at rest (E) equals its mass (m) times the speed of light (c) squared ($E=mc^2$). Ten years later his General Theory of Relativity was formulated, and he became the first modern scientist to achieve worldwide fame. He was the recipient of the 1921 Nobel Prize for Physics for his explanation of the photoelectric effect and 'for his services to Theoretical Physics'. Despite all his successes, however, he seemed to yearn for something more . . .

'If I had my life to live over again, I'd be a plumber.'

'If I had only known, I would have been a locksmith.'

'If I were not a physicist, I would probably be a musician. I often think in music. I live my daydreams in music. I see my life in terms of music . . . I get most joy in life out of music.'

'If my theory of relativity is proven successful, Germany will claim me as a German and France will declare that I am a citizen of the world. Should my theory prove untrue, France will say that I am a German and Germany will declare that I am a Jew.'

Brain Drain

- Einstein couldn't speak properly until he was nine years old, and so it was assumed he suffered from dyslexia.

- After Einstein's death his body was cremated, but his brain was preserved for scientific study – at least it was supposed to have been. In fact, after a Dr Harvey removed it during the autopsy, he took possession of it himself, and it wasn't seen again until 1978. Harvey later explained that he had wanted 'to find out, if possible, what was the source of his [Einstein's] intelligence, of his genius'.

> 'Stop quoting laws to us. We carry swords.'
> **Gnaeus Pompeius Magnus**

WAR: THE TOOLS OF THE TRADE

Mankind was at war almost as soon as he became civilized, but as it's not nice to throw stones, man invented some other things to throw and fire, including the bow and arrow, which was in use as long as 25,000 years ago. Man could now kill animals more efficiently, as well as humans, and could defend himself from attack. In fact, the bow and arrow has been ranked in importance with the discovery of speech and the ability to make fire.

Man liked to throw fire too: simple flame-throwers were standard military hardware in ancient Greece, and gasoline-fuelled flame-throwers were even used during the First World War.

In 213 BC, Archimedes saved Syracuse (for a time) from Roman conquest by means of the Archimedes Claw – a huge war machine that grasped the prow of ships and tipped them over.

The ancients knew that fighting was not always necessary in warfare. When the Persians laid siege to Pelusium, they used cats as shields. The Egyptians regarded certain animals, especially cats, as sacred, and did not dare to shoot their arrows for fear of wounding them.

When towns refused to surrender, a little germ warfare might be entertained. Throwing plague victims over the walls of besieged cities was one practice. In 1763, blankets infected with smallpox were sent to the Pontiac American Indians, which wiped them out.

From the reign of William the Conqueror (reigned 1066–87) to the sixteenth century, the longbow was England's principal weapon of national defence, allowing the English army to triumph against the French at Agincourt and Poitiers. Legend has it that before the Battle of Agincourt, the French threatened to cut off the English bowmen's fingers. Having won, the bowmen stuck their fingers up at the French to rub in their victory, and the two-finger insult stuck.

While in the employ of the Duke of Milan (between 1482 and 1499), Leonardo da Vinci drew up designs for many weapons including hand-grenades, machine-type guns, a primitive tank, and even a submarine.

Gunpowder was invented in China in about 700. Some nations took a little longer to realize its advantages – in the defeat of the Spanish Armada in 1588, 10,000 English troops were equipped with firearms, but the Spanish were armed with bows and arrows.

In 1864, Alfred Nobel's nitro-glycerine factory blew up, killing five people, including his brother. After that Nobel worked to invent a more stable explosive and came up with dynamite. (In actual fact, Nobel [1833–96] was a pacifist, and he had intended that his invention be used in engineering rather than in war.)

Although others had their doubts about artillery 'tractors', Sir Winston Churchill (1874–1965) ordered one to be built that was capable of crossing trenches. Thus, Royal Naval Air Service Lt W. G. Wilson and Mr W. Tritton came up with 'Mother', which rolled across Lord Salisbury's golf course in front of army experts. The initial order was for a hundred of them. Their codename was 'tanks'.

During the Second World War, on 6 August 1945, the US Army Air Force dropped an atomic bomb on Hiroshima, Japan, killing an estimated 140,000 people in the first use of a nuclear weapon in war.

On 30 October 1961, the USSR set off the largest nuclear explosion in history, detonating a bomb 2,600 times the strength of the Hiroshima bomb in a test over the Novaya Zemlya Islands, off Siberia.

Bum Shots

The Parthians of Central Asia were famous for being able to shoot backwards from a galloping horse, which is how we get the expression to deliver a Parthian (now 'parting') shot.

> 'You know you get a lot more with a kind word and a gun than you do with a kind word alone.'
> **Al Capone**

THE TIMES, THEY ARE EXPLODING

Alfred Nobel amassed vast personal wealth from his invention of safe explosives, detonating devices and his interests in oil. However, Nobel was a pacifist and feared that his inventions might be used against rather than for the good of mankind. Thus he left much of his fortune to funding a series of awards – one of them an accolade for peace – which are known as the Nobel Prizes.

A number of inventors of the atomic bomb were appalled at the havoc wreaked in Hiroshima and Nagasaki. In 1946, the Union of Concerned Scientists was formed as a protest against irresponsible progress. During the Second World War, J. Robert Oppenheimer (1904–67) was the scientific director of the Manhattan Project (the race to develop the first nuclear weapons) at the secret Los Alamos laboratory in New Mexico. After seeing the effects of his creation, however, Oppenheimer lobbied for international control of atomic energy and to avert the nuclear-arms race with the Soviet Union.

AFTERWORDS AND FALLOUT

'The real problem is in the hearts and minds of men. It is easier to denature plutonium than to denature the evil spirit of man.'
Albert Einstein

'My God, what have we done?'
**Robert Lewis, co-pilot of the B-29 bomber *Enola Gay*
over Hiroshima, 6 August 1945**

'Now I am become death, the destroyer of worlds.'
J. Robert Oppenheimer, 'the father of the atomic bomb'

'I know not with what weapons World War III will be fought, but World War IV will be fought with sticks and stones.'
Albert Einstein

'In nuclear war all men are cremated equal.'
Dexter Gordon

'We can bomb the world into pieces, but we can't bomb it into peace.'
Michael Franti

'ADVANCED' TECHNOLOGY

'The question of whether a computer can really think is as interesting
as the question of whether a submarine can really swim.'
Edsger Dijkstra

'Technological progress has merely provided us with more
efficient means for going backwards.'
Aldous Huxley

'The wireless telegraph is not difficult to understand. The ordinary
telegraph is like a very long cat. You pull the tail in New York, and it
meows in Los Angeles. The wireless is the same, only without the cat.'
Albert Einstein

'We live in a society exquisitely dependent on science and
technology, in which hardly anyone knows anything about
science and technology.'
Carl Sagan

'Assembling the maximum amount of information on the universe
can put an end to the world. As in the fable of the nine billion names
of God: when, thanks to the computer, we've been able to decline
them all, the world will end, and the stars will go out.'
Jean Baudrillard

'To err is human, but to really foul things up requires a computer.'
Farmers' Almanac, **1978**

Back to the Future

In 1863, Jules Verne (1828–1905) wrote a novel called *Paris in the 20th
Century* about a young man who lives in a world of skyscrapers, high-
speed trains, gas-powered automobiles, calculators, and a worldwide
communications network. His publisher thought the novel too
pessimistic – the young man cannot find happiness and comes to a
tragic end – and so the manuscript was put in a safe. It was discovered
by Verne's great-grandson in 1989 and was published in 1994.

> 'Anyone who has lived through an English winter can see the
> point of building Stonehenge to make the Sun come back.'
> **Alison Jolly**

BLOWING HOT AND COLD

Galileo Galilei knew that air expanded and cooled, and around 1593
he invented a primitive thermometer (a cylindrical tube in water),
but it didn't exactly work.

In 1709, Polish physicist Daniel Fahrenheit (1686–1736) invented an
alcohol thermometer that was to improve upon Galileo's first effort.
Five years later, he eclipsed his earlier invention with his mercury
thermometer. In 1715, he developed the Fahrenheit temperature
scale, which is still in use today. Fahrenheit's lowest temperature was
0°F, which he achieved by blending ice and salt, while the boiling
point of water was 212°F.

The metric centrigrade scale was devised by Anders Celsius
(1701–44), a Swedish professor of astronomy. His Celsius
thermometer appeared in 1742. Originally the boiling point on the
Celsius scale was 0°C and the freezing point was 100°C, but the
metric scale was later revised to the one we use today by a fellow
Swede, the botanist Carl von Linné (1707–78).

At the grand old age of ten, William Thomson (1824–1907) went to
Glasgow University. During his studies he discovered that heat can
only flow spontaneously from a hotter to a colder body (the second
law of thermodynamics). He also defined an absolute temperature
scale – absolute zero being 273.16°C; you can't get colder than that.
In 1892, Thomson entered the House of Lords and became Lord
Kelvin. The Kelvin scale is widely used by scientists today.

Going to Extremes

- The highest temperature on Earth was 58°C (136°F) in Libya in 1922.
- The lowest temperature on Earth was –89.6°C (–128.6°F) in
  Antarctica in 1983.
- The centre of the Sun is about 15,000,000°C (27,000,000°F).

FLY ME TO THE MOON

On 12 April 1961, Lt Yuri Gagarin (1934–68) of the Soviet Union
became the first man in space, piloting *Vostock I* at an altitude of
327 km (203 miles).

On 20 July 1969 Americans Neil Armstrong (b.1930) and Edwin
'Buzz' Aldrin (b.1930) became the first men to walk on the Moon.
Just 20 seconds worth of fuel remained when *Apollo 11*'s lunar
module landed.

Skylab, the first American space station, fell to Earth in thousands of
pieces in 1979. Fortunately most of it landed in the sea.

The rocket that launched *Apollo 12* in November 1969 was struck by
lightning just after lift-off, temporarily disabling all onboard systems.

On 16 October 1976, the Soviet *Soyuz 23* capsule broke through the
surface of a frozen lake when landing back on Earth.

In February 1986, the Soviets launched the *Mir* orbiting system, and
in 1997, the US astronaut David Wolf was allowed to vote for
Houston's Mayor while on board.

On 28 January 1986, the US space programme suffered its first in-
flight fatalities, when the space shuttle *Challenger* was destroyed 73
seconds after launch, with the loss of all seven crew members. A
second shuttle, *Columbia,* broke apart on re-entry on 1 February 2003.

Right now you are travelling in space at 107,343 kph (66,700 mph).
This is the speed at which the Earth orbits the Sun.

Strange, But True

An astronaut can be up to 5 cm (2 inches) taller returning from space.
The cartilage disks in the spine expand in the absence of gravity.

IS THERE ANYBODY OUT THERE?

'Men fancied there might be other men upon Mars, perhaps inferior
to themselves and ready to welcome a missionary enterprise.'
H. G. Wells in 1897

'I don't think God put me on this planet to judge others.
I think He put me on this planet to gather specimens and take
them back to my home planet.'
Jack Handy

'The surest sign that intelligent life exists elsewhere in the
universe is that it has never tried to contact us.'
Bill Watterson

'Calculations of the probability of other inhabited planets in our
galaxy are rather meaningless at this stage of our knowledge of the
origin of life. But in the framework of the cosmological principle we
should assume that there is at least one inhabited planet per galaxy.'
Michael Rowan-Robinson

'We hope someday, having solved the problems we face,
to join a community of galactic civilizations.'
President Jimmy Carter in 1977

'Sometimes I think we're alone. Sometimes I think we're not.
In either case, the prospect is staggering!'
Arthur C. Clarke

'I thought, "The Martians have arrived!" but then I realized
that I was looking at pollen slightly out of focus.'
Patrick Moore

'After one look at this planet, any visitor from outer space
would say, "I WANT TO SEE THE MANAGER."'
William S. Burroughs

'The only truly alien planet is Earth.'
J. G. Ballard

THOUGHTS ON TIME TRAVEL

'A seminar on Time Travel will be held two weeks ago.'
Anonymous

Some scientists now believe that if we were to travel back in time and change history, we would not change the future of this universe, but would create a parallel universe.

A rocket explorer named Wright,
Once travelled much faster than light.
He set out one day, in a relative way,
And returned on the previous night.
Anonymous

NOTHINGNESS

'A vacuum is a hell of a lot better than some of the stuff that nature replaces it with.'
Tennessee Williams

'Eternal nothingness is fine if you happen to be dressed for it.'
Woody Allen

'God made everything out of nothing, but the nothingness shows through.'
Paul Valéry

'Nature abhors a vacuum.'
François Rabelais

> 'For all things come from earth, and all things
> end by becoming earth.'
> **Xenophanes**

GONE AWAY: SOME EXTINCT ANIMALS AND BIRDS

Dinosaurs	Woolly mammoths
Sabre-toothed tigers	Dodos
Tasmanian devils	Great auks
Moas	Sea minks

- There are about 4,000 mammals on the planet, a fifth of which are under threat, as also are a third of amphibians and a quarter of the world's coniferous trees.

- Since life began, about 99 per cent of the Earth's species have disappeared. Today, the extinction rate is increasing rapidly as a result of human interference in natural ecosystems. Currently, evolution generates new species far more slowly than the rate of extinction.

ACTS OF GOD VI: LIGHTNING

In 1752, the US statesman, inventor and scientist Benjamin Franklin (1706–90) conducted an experiment with a kite in a thunderstorm and invented the lightning rod (the kite had a metal key attached to it). Thanks to him, US cities acquired lightning conductors, so that people didn't have to worry about their homes being struck by lightning any more. However, certain members of the Church weren't happy about it, as they believed people were interfering with the wrath of God. In France, the citizens of Saint-Omer actually filed a suit against M. Vissery de Bois-Valé for putting up a lightning conductor, believing that it was a blasphemous act for which they would all be punished.

THE END IS NIGH

Since mankind evolved he has worried about his future. There have
been hundreds of apocryphal theories and portents of our doom.
However, for now at any rate, our universe, our planet and ourselves
are still here.

In 968 an eclipse was interpreted as a prelude to the end of the world
by the army of the German Emperor Otto III.

If people had been better informed of the year, no doubt widespread
panic would have ensued on 1 January 1000 – the date predicted by
some Christians to be the end of the world. As the date approached,
anxious Christians fought wars with neighbouring 'heathens' in an
attempt to convert them before the return of Christ. Whether they did
so to save pagan souls or to earn brownie points, I can't say. However,
the Church was happy to accept the possessions of those who thought
they would have no further need of them. People who complained
afterwards were branded heretics.

Martin Luther (1483–1546) predicted that the world would end no
later than the year 1600.

The English clergy once predicted that the year 1666 would be the end
of things. Londoners believed them when the Great Fire started in that
year, following on from the Great Plague. Life went on, however.
Nostradamus supposedly predicted that July 1999 would be the day
of doom. His followers had to have a little rethink by August.

The Y2k bug added a note of nervousness to millennium celebrations
but in the end didn't bug us after all.

'Why worry about the world coming to an end today.
It's already tomorrow in Australia.'
Charles Schultz

> '"God is dead" – Nietzsche.
> "Nietzsche is dead" – God.'
> **Anonymous**

TOMBSTONE EPITAPHS

'Here lies John Timothy Snow,
who died fighting for a lady's honor.
(She wanted to keep it.)'
Tombstone in Arizona

'Beneath this grassy mound now rests
One Edgar Oscar Earl,
Who to another hunter looked
Exactly like a squirrel.'
Tombstone in England

'Here lies Ann Mann;
She lived an old maid and
She died an Old Mann.'
On a gravestone at Bath Abbey, England

'Here lies Jan Smith, wife of Thomas Smith, marble cutter.
This monument was erected by her husband as a tribute
to her memory and a specimen of his work.
Monuments of this same style are $250.'
Gravestone inscription

> 'If you would not be forgotten as soon as you are dead
> and rotten, either write things worth reading, or do
> things worth the writing.'
> **Benjamin Franklin**

THOUGHTS ON HEAVEN AND HELL

'Maybe this world is another planet's hell.'
Aldous Huxley

'Hell hath no limits nor is circumscrib'd
In one self place, where we are is Hell,
And where Hell is, there must we ever be.
And to be short, when all the world dissolves,
And every creature shall be purified,
All places shall be hell that are not heaven.'
Christopher Marlowe

'Repent ye: for the kingdom of heaven is at hand.'
Matthew 3:2

'Go to Heaven for the climate, Hell for the company.'
Mark Twain

'The future is like Heaven – everyone exalts it,
but no one wants to go there now.'
James Arthur Baldwin

Around 1200, the Catholic Church adopted Aristotle's cosmology, which included corrupt Earth, perfect Heaven, and most corrupt Hell. To think otherwise was considered heresy.

Heavenly motion was considered to be in circles. A perfect shape was circles within circles.

In *Inferno*, the first volume of *The Divine Comedy*, the Italian poet Dante (1265–1321) wrote about descending the nine circles to Hell and ascending the celestial spheres to God.

Strange, But True

In eighteenth-century London you could purchase insurance against going to Hell.

THE END OF THE WORLD AS WE KNOW IT

Theories abound about the end of the world, the destruction of Earth and the likely future of the Universe – here are a few possibilities.

STRETCHING THINGS A BIT TOO FAR

The American astronomer Edwin Powell Hubble (1889–1953) is noted for discovering that there are other galaxies beyond the Milky Way, and also for his findings on the growth of our Universe. Scientists once believed that the expansion was slowing down, but now think that, with the help of some dark energy, our Universe is actually increasing in size even faster than before. If the expansion continues for ever then the Universe is destined for the Big Freeze, gradually pulled apart into a wasteland of dying stars and black holes. If the stretching stops, the bad news is that we still get to freeze. The good news is that we will have time on our side, as it isn't due to happen for some billions or even trillions of years.

IN THE GRIP OF THE RIP

If you were worried about the rip in your jeans, try this for size. In a far-off time – to be strictly accurate, 20 billion years from now – galaxies will be separated from each other, solar systems will be gravitationally unbound, stars and planets will come apart, and atoms will be destroyed. That's the Big Rip.

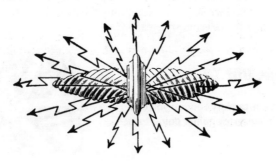

METEOR A-COMING – TAKE COVER

Lots of meteors pay a visit to Earth's atmosphere every day, and only a few survive the effect of atmospheric friction. However, astronomers have predicted that asteroid (29075) 1950 DA will come very close to Earth or indeed collide with our planet on 16 March 2880. Could this be the end of life as we know it?

HELLO SUNTANS

Over the years, thanks to high levels of pollution and the use of ozone-destroying products, we've managed to make a nice 'hole' in the sky somewhere above the Arctic Circle. The experts who discovered it thought their instruments had gone wrong when they measured ozone levels, but though scientists are trying to mend the hole so the Sun's powerful rays won't hurt us too much in the short term, in the long-term, however, we might all get frazzled.

GOODBYE SUNTANS

The Sun is about 4.6 billion years old and has already used up almost half of the hydrogen supply in its core. When it runs out of these reserves in about 5 billion years, it will expand into a red giant (dying star), while the Earth will not be able to exist without the Sun's rays. However, we might not even get that far. According to some experts the Sun is getting hotter and in less than a billion years, Earth might be too hot a spot for us in which we can safely live.

THE BIG CRUNCH OR GNAB GIB

It may be the case that when our Universe has stretched as far as it can, it will begin to spring back upon itself. It will shrink until galaxies start colliding in the Big Crunch or Gnab Gib (Big Bang spelt backwards), and all that will be left of our Universe will be a very large black hole.

So perhaps we should really make the most of it, before time is well and truly called on our finite existence . . .

WORM-HOLING OUT OF IT

Looking on the bright side, it may be possible that one day in the future we could escape to another Universe. We just have to find a suitable wormhole (or gateway) to a parallel dimension. There may be an infinite number of these, and they may be close by. The trouble is it will take some giant steps, a lot of energy, and a good deal of swotting up on quantum gravity and string theory, before we can really find out if this idea is viable. Fingers crossed, eh?

THE END

> 'This is not the end. It is not even the
> beginning of the end.
> But, it is, perhaps, the end of the beginning.'
> **Sir Winston Churchill**

SOURCES, CREDITS AND FURTHER READING

BOOKS

Arnold, Nick, *Deadly Diseases* (Hippo, 2000)

Arnold, Nick, *Horrible Science: Deadly Diseases* (Scholastic Ltd, 2000)

Balchin, Jon, *100 Scientists Who Changed The World* (Arcturus, 2003)

Batchelor, John, and Lowe, Malcolm V., *The Complete Encyclopedia of Flight 1848–1939* (Rebo International, 2004)

Blake, Stephen, and John, Andrew, *The Little Book of Great Ideas* (Michael O'Mara Books Ltd, 2001)

Carter, Philip, and Russell, Ken, *The Complete Book of Fun Maths* (John Wiley & Sons Ltd, 2004)

Cawthorne, Nigel, *100 Disasters That Shook The World* (Arcturus, 2004)

Corbishley, Mike, *Timelines of the Ancient World* (Hodder Wayland, 1995)

De Bono, Edward, (ed.) *Eureka!: An Illustrated History of Inventions From the Wheel to the Computer* (Thames and Hudson Ltd, 1974)

The Good News Bible (Collins, 1976)

Held, Robert, *Inquisition* (Avon & Arnold, 1991)

Hewitt, Sally, *The Great Fire of London* (Franklin Watts, 2004)

Locke, Ian, *Cool Cars* (Macmillan, 1998)

Roberts, J. M., *The Penguin History of the World* (Penguin Books, 1995)

Stewart, Robert, *The Illustrated Encyclopedia of Historical Facts* (Simon & Schuster Ltd, 1992)

Taber, C. W., *Lippencotts Home Manuals; The Business of the Household* (1918)

Vaughan, John G., and others, *The New Oxford Book of Food Plants* (Oxford University Press, 1997)

Walker, Richard D. and others, *Inventions That Changed The World* (Reader's Digest, 1996)

Washington, George, *Rules of Civility & Decent Behaviour in Company and Conversation: A Book of Etiquette* (Beaver Press, 1971)

ARTICLES

'Ancient Egyptian Alcohol', Caroline Seawright, *Modern Drunkard Magazine*, 2004
'Commercial Agriculture: Facts and Figures', J. Robert Hatherill, Ph.D
'Death on a Grand Scale', Cynthia M. Piccolo
'Great Moments in Toilet Paper History', Buck Wold, 11 April 2001
'Having the Last Laugh', Arlene F. Harder, MA, MFT
'History of Public Toilets', Bindeswar Pathak, Ph.D., D. Litt.
'Some facts about Anthrax', Stephen B. Blezinger
    (www.cattletoday.com)
'Roman Numerals, History and Use', Paul Lewis, 1999–2001
'The Origins of Language', Dr. C. George Boeree
'Time Travel: Shaping the Future', Neil Johnson (www.bbc.co.uk)

WEBSITES

en.wikipedia.org
www.abcnews.com
www.askoxford.com
www.bankofengland.co.uk/history
www.bbc.co.uk
www.bible-history.com
www.bog-standard.org
www.cattletoday.com
www.cobritishfarming.org.uk
www.cseindia.org
www.es.ucsb.edu
www.fashionera.com
www.historicuk.com
www.greenleafcompost.com
www.littlemonkeymurals.com
www.millionminute.com
www.minerals.usgs.gov/west/morefun.shtml
www.moorlandschool.co.uk/earth/earths_structure.htm
www.nationalgeographic.com
www.obliquity.com/skyeye/
www.painforum.com/en/1/throughtheages.html
www.perfumes.com
www.plumbingworld.com
www.quotegarden.com/religion.html
www.scienceinthebox.com
www.sharontylerherbst.com/trivia.htm
www.toiletpaperworld.com
www.volcanoworld.org
www.yourDictionary.com